100
False
Bible
Prophecies

Robert Collins

This book is dedicated
to every Bible believer
who ever asked
their minister, pastor, preacher or priest
sincere, direct factual questions
about the Bible
and did not receive
sincere, direct, factual answers.

Contents

Introduction

Is the Bible the inspired word of God? Multitudes of Bible scholars have spent their lives trying to answer this question through archaeology, study of ancient languages, textual analysis and apologetics.

The Bible provides its own standard for determining whether something is God's word. "How shall we know the word which the Lord hath not spoken? When a prophet speaketh in the name of the Lord, if the thing follow not, nor come to pass, that is the thing which the Lord hath not spoken, but the prophet hath spoken it presumptuously: thou shalt not be afraid of him" (Deuteronomy 18:21-22).

If the Bible's prophecies can be proven to have been made before the events that they predicted and then authentically fulfilled, this would provide powerful evidence that there is something uniquely supernatural about it.

But if some of the Bible's many prophecies can be proven false, then according to the Bible's own standard of proof, the Bible cannot be the word of God. In that case, every Bible believer would have to make a personal decision about what parts of the Bible they could or could not believe. In short, every Bible believer would have to treat the Bible like they would treat any other book.

This book examines some of the prophecies in the Bible to see whether they came true. The answer is clear, and will be life-changing for many Bible believers who have been asking honest questions of their spiritual leaders and not receiving answers that satisfied their minds.

Robert Collins, March 2009

False Prophecy #1

In Matthew 12:40, Jesus said, "For as Jonas [Jonah] was three days and three nights in the whale's belly, so shall the Son of Man be three days and three nights in the heart of the earth." (See also Jonah 1:17.) This prophecy is repeated in various forms in Matthew 16:4 and Luke 11:29-30. This is a very precise prophecy attributed to Jesus himself concerning his own resurrection; and it is demonstrably false from the Bible itself.

The Gospels make very definite statements that Jesus died on a Friday afternoon and was raised around dawn on the following Sunday morning. This belief is foundational to Christian theology and is the basis for Good Friday and Easter rituals celebrated every year.

From Friday afternoon to Sunday morning is at most 40 hours, not three days and nights. Some argue this did include portions of three days, since Jewish days are counted from sundown to sundown, which stretches the facts but may appear plausible to some people.

However, there is just no way to get "three nights" out of this. The Bible says that Jesus died on Friday shortly before the Sabbath, which began at sundown (Mark 15:37-47, Luke 23:46-56, John 19:31-42). The Bible also says that Jesus was raised around sunrise on Sunday morning (Matthew 28:1-7, Mark 16:1-6, Luke 24:1-6, John 20:1). Friday afternoon to Sunday morning is <u>two</u> nights.

False Prophecy #2

Matthew 12:38-40 contains another false prophecy. It says, "Then certain of the scribes and of the Pharisees answered, saying, Master, we would see a sign from thee. But he [Jesus] answered and said unto them, 'An evil and adulterous generation seeketh after a sign; and there shall *no sign* be given to it, but the sign of the prophet Jonas For as Jonas [Jonah] was three days and three nights in the whale's belly, so shall the Son of Man be three days and three nights in the heart of the earth'". This same idea is repeated in Matthew 16:4, Mark 8:11-12 and Luke 11:29. In these passages, Jesus very clearly predicted that only one sign would be given: his resurrection.

But the Bible says that Jesus performed many signs. Greek word translated "sign" in Matthew 12:38-39 and the other verses referenced above is, "semeion."

<u>Many people saw the signs:</u>

John 6:2, "a great multitude followed him [Jesus], because they

1

saw his miracles [semeion].”

John 6:14,”Then those men, when they had seen the miracle [semeion] that Jesus did, said, This is of a truth that prophet”

John 12:17-18 “The people therefore that were with him [Jesus] when he called Lazarus out of his grave, and raised him from the dead, bare record. For this cause the people also met him, for that they heard that he had done this miracle [semeion]”.

Many people believed in Jesus because of the signs:

John 2:23, “many believed in his name, when they saw the miracles [semeion] which he did”

John 3:2, “Rabbi , we know that thou art a teacher come from God: for no man can do these miracles [semeion] that thou doest, except God be with him”.

John 4:48-54, “Then said Jesus unto him, Except ye see signs [semeion] and wonders, ye will not believe. The nobleman saith unto him, Sir, come down ere my child die ... Jesus saith unto him, Go thy way; thy son liveth. And the man believed the word that Jesus had spoken unto him ... his servants met him, and told him, saying, Thy son liveth ... So the father knew that it was at the same hour, in the which Jesus said unto him, Thy son liveth, and himself believed, and his whole house. This is again the second miracle [semeion] that Jesus did”.

John 7:31, “many of the people believed on him, and said, When Christ cometh, will he do more miracles [semeion] than these which this man hath done?”

John 10:41-42, “many resorted unto him, and said, John [the Baptist] did no miracle [semeion]: but all things that John spake of this man were true And many believed on him there”.

John 11:45 says that after Jesus raised Lazarus from the dead “many of the Jews which came to Mary [Lazarus’ sister], and had seen the things which Jesus did, believed on him”

Many of Jesus’ signs were seen by unbelievers:

John 6:26, “Ye seek me, not because ye saw the miracles [semeion] but because ye did eat of the loaves, and were filled”.

John 12:37, “though he had done so many miracles [semeion] before them, yet they believed not on him”

Acts 2:22 , “Ye men of Israel, hear these words; Jesus of Nazareth, a man approved of God among you by miracles [a different Greek word:

2

dunamis] and wonders and signs [semeion], which God did by him in the midst of you, as ye yourselves also know".

False Prophecy #3

Matthew 2:23 says, "And he [Joseph] came and dwelt in a city called Nazareth: that it might be fulfilled which was spoken by the prophets, He shall be called a Nazarene". The Old Testament contains <u>no</u> prophecy that the Messiah would be a Nazarene or would be from Nazareth. So Matthew 2:23 is not just a false prophecy; it is a fraudulent prophecy. The author of Matthew simply manufactured a prophecy and reported that it had been "fulfilled", although no such prophecy actually existed.

Some people have argued that the "prophets" in this verse were not Biblical prophets; they were other prophets of God that were not recorded in the Bible. This so-called explanation deprives this passage of all predictive, evidential or apologetic value. If you are going to use a prophecy to prove that God could predict the future and/or prove that someone was the Messiah because he fulfilled a prophecy, then there has to be some evidence that the prophecy was made before it was reported to be fulfilled. That evidence does not exist for Matthew 2:23.

False Prophecy #4

John 13:18 says that Jesus claimed that Judas' betrayal fulfilled Old Testament prophecy. "I speak not of you all: I know whom I have chosen: but that the scripture may be fulfilled, He that eateth bread with me hath lifted up his heel against me". This is a quote from Psalm 41:9, "Yea, mine own familiar friend, in whom I trusted, which did eat of my bread, hath lifted up his heel against me."

The problem is that Psalm 41 cannot possibly be talking about Jesus Christ. The very next verse, Psalm 41:10, says, "But thou, O Lord, be merciful unto me". Psalm 41:4 says, "I said, Lord, be merciful unto me: heal my soul; for I have sinned against thee".

False Prophecy #5

Matthew 2:12-18 describes what many Christians call The Slaughter of the Innocents[1] , Herod's mass murder of all of the male children in Bethlehem who were 2 years old or younger. It then claims that this massacre was foretold by Old Testament prophecy, "In Rama was there a voice heard, lamentation, and weeping, and great mourning, Rachel weeping for her children, and would not be comforted, because they are not".

(Jeremiah 31:15).

This "prophecy" is as incorrect as a prophecy can be. First, Jeremiah 31:15 was not referring to murder. The surrounding verses make it clear that Jeremiah was referring to children who had been carried away into exile. For example, the very next two verses (Jeremiah 31:16-17) say twice that the weeping mothers will be comforted because their children will come again to their own land.

Second, Bethlehem was the city of David (Luke 2:4 and 2:11). David was descended from Leah, not Rachel (Matthew 1:2-6, Luke 3:31-33, Genesis 29:32-30:1). The descendants of David were not mentioned in this "prophecy" in the book of Jeremiah.

Third, Jeremiah 31:15 says that this would occur in "Rama", not Bethlehem. Bethlehem is located 5 miles south of Jerusalem, in the land of the tribe of Judah. The Old Testament lists three cities named "Rama": one in the land of the tribe of Benjamin (Joshua 18:21-25), another in Naphtali (Joshua 19:32-36) and yet another in Ephraim (1 Samuel 1:1, 7:15-17), all of which were located several hours or even several days journeys north of Jerusalem. Three verses in Jeremiah chapter 31 specifically refer to "Ephraim". The town of "Rama" in Ephraim was located about a day's journey north of Bethlehem.

Finally, Jeremiah, supposedly writing around 600 years before the Gospel of Matthew says that Jesus was born, claimed that his "prophecy" would be fulfilled soon after it was made. Jeremiah 31:16-17 clearly says that mothers will be comforted because their children will return, indicating that all of this will be fulfilled within a human lifespan.

So this "prophecy" was wrong in 4 ways:

Jeremiah Predicted	Matthew Reported
Children kidnapped/deported	Children murdered
Descendants of Rachel	Descendants of Leah
In Rama	In Bethlehem
Less than 1 lifetime after 600 BCE	4 BCE or a few years earlier

Another strong evidence that the Jeremiah prophecy was either wrong or hopelessly vague (or that Matthew chapter 2 is a complete myth) is that not one person in Bethlehem used their knowledge of Jeremiah's prophecy to protect their children from death. If you were a parent and learned of the slightest hint that someone was going to kill your child, you would immediately get that child out of town and into a safe hiding place.

4

Bethlehem was overwhelmingly Hebrew; they knew their Old Testaments. Yet God had to warn Joseph and the wise men in dreams. Even when God himself warned them of personal danger, they did not sound the alarm to the rest of Bethlehem, which went unwarned, and so those poor little boys fell victim to mass murder.

It gets worse. Matthew 2:12-18's false claim of fulfilled prophecy pales beside the moral turpitude displayed by God if this passage is literal history. God protected Jesus (Matthew 2:13-14) and the wise men (Matthew 2:12). God had the power to protect all of those little babies and toddlers (Matthew 28:18), but he did not.

God claimed that he knew hundreds of years in advance that this massacre was going to happen, and still did nothing to prevent it. If you have a few hundred years advance warning, you can prevent just about any crime, particularly if you happen to be omnipotent (Matthew 19:26).

Job 36:15 promises that God "delivereth the poor in his affliction". Psalm 34:19 promises "Many are the afflictions of the righteous: but the Lord delivereth him out of them all". Psalm 18:27 promises that God "wilt save the afflicted people". But these poor innocent Hebrew babies and toddlers were murdered anyway while God watched (Proverbs 15:3, Jeremiah 23:24).

If you know in advance that someone is going to murder a lot of people and you don't try to prevent it, it is a crime in all civilized nations. In 1995, Timothy McVeigh detonated a bomb very close to a child care center located in a federal building in Oklahoma City; 168 people were killed, including 15 children. Michael Fourtier knew in advance that McVeigh was going to do this, but Fourtier did not tell police in advance, so Fourtier was sentenced to many years in prison.

If a human knows in advance of a mass murder and does not try to prevent it, it is a felony. But if God claims to do the same thing, Bible believers think that it is a miraculous prophecy.

It gets even worse. Many commentators estimate that at most a few dozen male babies and toddlers were murdered in Herod's "Slaughter of the Innocents" because Bethlehem was a small village. Since no ancient historian mentions this slaughter, including the first century Jewish historian Josephus, their silence indicates that the number of victims would have been small enough that it did not attract widespread attention (assuming it did actually happen). The murder of even one little boy is a heinous crime, so Herod's acts have earned him a well-deserved designation as one of history's most evil sociopaths.

But Herod's slaughter was miniscule compared to God's many slaughters of children. In Numbers 31:17, God through Moses commanded, "Now therefore kill every male among the little ones". Although the Bible does not give the exact number of boys who were murdered, Numbers 31:35 says that they Israelites saved 32,000 female virgins for themselves, so a similar number of male virgins were exterminated.

In a separate mass murder, God commanded "utterly destroy all that they have, and spare them not; but slay both man and woman, infant and suckling" (1 Samuel 15:3). Envision in your mind what actually happened when the Israelites carried out God's command - babies were ripped from the breasts of mothers pleading for mercy for their children, then mothers and babies were murdered en masse, if the Bible is historically accurate.

God commanded his largest mass murder in Deuteronomy 22:16-17. "Of the cities of these people, which the Lord thy God doth give thee for an inheritance, thou shalt save alive nothing that breatheth, But thou shalt utterly destroy them; namely, the Hittites, and the Amorites, the Canaanites, and the Perizzites, the Hivites, and the Jebusites; as the Lord thy God hath commanded thee." If the Bible is true, then the Israelites very literally obeyed this command in Joshua chapters 10-11, genocidally exterminating many millions of people, including enormous numbers of children.

False Prophecy #6

Matthew 1:11-12 names Jechonias as one of Jesus' ancestors. "Josias begat Jechonias and his brethren, about the time they were carried away to Babylon, And after they were brought to Babylon, Jechonias begat Salathiel". But Jeremiah 22:30 prophesies that the Messiah cannot be descended from Jechonias, "Thus saith the Lord, Write ye this man childless [Judah's king Jeconiah, see Jeremiah 22:24 and 22:28], a man that shall not prosper in his days: for no man of his seed shall prosper, sitting upon the throne of David, and ruling any more in Judah."

Jesus himself said he believed that he was king of the Jews (Matthew 27:11, 28:18, Mark 15:2, Luke 23:3, John 1:49-51). So did his Apostles (Matthew 21:4-5, John 12:13-15). As for the throne of David, an angel said, "He [Jesus] shall be great, and shall be called the Son of the Highest: and the Lord God shall give unto him the throne of his father David" (Luke 1:32, see also Isaiah 9:6-7). But if Jeremiah was correct, no ruler of Israel, sitting on the throne of David, could have Jeconiah as an ancestor.

Some may argue that it does not matter that Matthew's genealogy includes Jechonias because Jesus was not biologically descended from Joseph. He was biologically descended from Mary, and that the genealogy through Mary is provided in Luke. This is a completely inadequate "explanation" for three reasons. **(1)** It admits that Matthew's genealogy is irrelevant. **(2)** Luke's genealogy never mentions Mary or any other woman. So there is no basis for arguing that it is actually Mary's genealogy. **(3)** Luke's genealogy also has insurmountable problems. The author of Luke traces Jesus' ancestry through David's son Nathan, which contradicts 1 Chronicles 22:9-10: "Behold, a son shall be born to thee ... his name shall be [Nathan's brother] Solomon ... he shall be my son, and I will be his father; and I will establish throne of his kingdom over Israel for ever."

False Prophecy #7

Matthew 1:23 quotes the prophecy of Isaiah 7:14. "Behold, a virgin shall be with child, and shall bring forth a son, and they shall call his name Emmanuel, which being interpreted is, God with us." This book will describe three problems with this prophecy. Problems #1 and #2 prove that the prophecy cannot be talking about Jesus Christ. Problem #3 demonstrates that the prophecy is so vague that it has no predictive value.

Problem #1: Matthew 1:23 misrepresents this Old Testament prophecy. Isaiah 7:14 very clearly did <u>not</u> prophesy a sinless divine Messiah to be born in the distant future. To see that Matthew 1:23 is wrong, we need look no farther than the very next two verses after Isaiah 7:14, which clearly show that this passage cannot possibly be talking about Jesus Christ. Isaiah 7:15-16 says, "Butter and honey shall he eat, that he may know to refuse the evil, and choose the good. For before the child shall know to refuse the evil, and choose the good, the land that thou abhorrest shall be forsaken of both her kings."

This passage cannot be talking about Jesus Christ because there was never a time "before" Jesus knew "to refuse the evil and choose the good". According to the Bible, Jesus is God (Colossians 2:9, John 10:30) and Jesus does not change (Hebrews 13:8).

This passage cannot be talking about Jesus Christ because Isaiah 7:14-16 gives a definite time period for Emmanuel's infancy and childhood. This "prophecy" says that two kings will be removed from power and/or their lands will be deserted before Immanuel is old enough to choose evil or good. These kings are specifically named in Isaiah chapter 7 - Syria's king Rezin (Isaiah 7:8) and Israel/Samaria/Ephraim's king Pekah son of Rema-

7

liah (Isaiah 7:9 and 7:1).

The Bible says that Rezin was killed around 740 BCE (2 Kings 16:9), so was Pekah (2 Kings 15:30). At about the same time, the king of Assyria deported all of the people in Damascus to Kir (2 Kings 16:9), an Assyrian district between the Caspian and Black seas. About 9 years afterwards, the king of Assyria deported all of Israel (i.e., all of the tribes except Judah, Benjamin and Levi) to various Assyrian cities (2 Kings 17:6). All of these events happened over 700 years before Jesus was born, if the Bible is historically accurate.

Problem #2: There is no other place in the entire New Testament where Jesus is called Emmanuel or Immanuel. Many people have been named Emmanuel (e.g., the philosopher Emmanuel Kant), but Jesus was not one of them.

The name Jesus does not mean "God with us". "Jesus" means "savior" or "God saves". The name "Jesus" is derived from the name "Joshua", which means "Jehovah saves". In ancient Greek Bible manuscripts, the names "Jesus" and "Joshua" are identical; for examples, see Acts 7:45 and Hebrews 4:8 in the King James Bible.

"Jesus" was a frequently used Jewish name in ancient times. One of Paul's disciples named "Jesus" is mentioned in Colossians 4:11. Josephus[2], the first century Jewish historian, mentions Jesus brother of Onias, Jesus son of Ananus, Jesus also called Jason, Jesus son of Apphias, Jesus son of Gamaliel, Jesus son of Damniel, Jesus son of Gamala, Jesus son of Saphat, and Jesus son of Thebuthus.

The Greek word translated "call" in Matthew 1:23 is, "kaleo"; the Greek word translated "name" in this verse is "onoma". So Matthew 1:23 reads, "they shall call [kaleo] his name [onoma] Emmanuel". But an angel commanded that he be named Jesus. "She shall bring forth a son, and thou shalt call [kaleo] his name [onoma] Jesus" (Matthew 1:21). So Joseph named him Jesus. "And [Joseph] knew her not till she had brought forth her firstborn son: and he called [kaleo] his name [onoma] Jesus." (Matthew 1:25, see also Luke 1:31 and Luke 2:21).

Problem #3: The Hebrew word translated "virgin" in Isaiah 7:14 in the KJB is "almah", which actually means "young woman", not "young woman who has never had sex". The Hebrew word for "virgin" is "bethulah" (see Genesis 24:16).

Anyone can predict that an unnamed young woman would have a child and have that prediction fulfilled without any supernatural help. Predicting a child's name can easily become a self-fulfilling prophecy. Besides, Jesus was named Jesus, not Emmanuel. (See Problem #1 above.)

False Prophecy #8

Matthew 2:14-15 says that Joseph took Jesus to Egypt "that it might be fulfilled which was spoken of the Lord by the prophet, saying, 'Out of Egypt have I called my son'".

This is a quote from Hosea 11:1-2 in the Old Testament. "When Israel was a child, then I loved him, and called my son out of Egypt. As they called them, so they went from them: they sacrificed unto Baalim, and burned incense to graven images."

It is difficult to imagine a more clear statement that this passage was talking about Israel, not the sinless Messiah, unless you want to believe that Jesus sacrificed unto Baalim, and burned incense to graven images.

False Prophecy #9

In Matthew 5:18, Jesus said, "For verily I say unto you, till heaven and earth pass, one jot or one tittle shall in no wise pass from the law, till all be fulfilled". This prophecy contradicts prophecies made by other Bible verses in two distinct ways. It also contains another prediction that is demonstrably untrue.

Contradiction #1: Matthew 5:18 says that the earth will "pass". This belief is repeated in Luke 21:33, where Jesus predicted, "Heaven and Earth shall pass away." But other verses in the Bible say that the earth will last forever. Ecclesiastes 1:4 says, "One generation passeth away, and another generation cometh: but the earth abideth for ever". Psalm 104:5 says, "[God] Who laid the foundations of the earth, that it should not be removed for ever". Psalm 78:69 says, "He [God] built his sanctuary like high palaces, like the earth which he hath established for ever".

Contradiction #2: This verse says that not "one jot or one tittle" shall pass from the law until two things happen: (A) heaven and earth pass and (B) all be fulfilled. Theologians have argued about the meaning of "all be fulfilled" for almost 2000 years without reaching an agreement. But the meaning of "till heaven and earth pass" is very clear, and it is also very clear that it has not happened. Even so, few Christians feel the need to undergo ritual circumcision, keep kosher or observe a Saturday sabbath, and none of them do any of the ritual sacrifices required by Old Testament Law.

False prediction: These words of Jesus predict that not "one jot or one tittle" shall pass from Old Testament law until the earth is destroyed. "Jot" and "tittle" are details smaller than individual characters. They are portions of individual Hebrew characters similar to crossing a "t" or dotting an "i" in English.

The earth is still here, but modern scholarship knows of hundreds of ancient and medieval Hebrew manuscripts which differ from each other in enormous numbers of ways. There is even a whole discipline of Biblical scholarship, "Textual Analysis", devoted to trying to figure out what the "originals" looked like based on manuscripts which are separated from the "originals" by hundreds of years, and for some passages, over 1300 years. Although these scholars do agree on some passages, they do not agree on every "jot and tittle" of all of them. The number of variations between manuscripts is so large that no one has an exact number, although many Bible scholars estimate the number of variations to be in the tens or hundreds of thousands[3]. No Bible scholar even claims that they know which texts are identical to the originals. Therefore, the knowledge of every "jot and tittle" of the Law of Moses has been lost to modern Bible believers.

This is very much in contrast to some other bodies of ancient law. For example, Hammurabi reigned over Babylon no later than the time that conservative Bible scholars believe that Isaac and Jacob lived (1700 BCE or earlier). We have a copy of over 3800 lines of text containing 282 of his laws, on a 7-foot high stone column on display at the Louvre in Paris, France. This column is topped by a bas-relief carving showing Hammurabi receiving these laws directly from the god Shemesh, and is believed to date from the lifetime of Hammurabi himself.

False Prophecy #10

In Matthew 5:22 Jesus predicted, "whosoever shall say 'Thou fool', shall be in danger of Hell fire." The Greek word translated "fool" in Matthew 5:22 is "moros". Jesus called people "moros" in Matthew 23:17 and 23:19. So if Jesus was telling the truth in Matthew 5:22, he himself is in danger of Hell fire. But Christians all believe that Jesus was sinless (1 Peter 1:19).

False Prophecy #11

Proverbs 16:7 predicts, "When a man's ways please the Lord, he maketh even his enemies to be at peace with him." The Hebrew word translated "enemies" in Proverbs 16:7 is "oyeb". Other Bible verses say very clearly that people who follow God will have many enemies [oyeb] who were definitely not at peace with them.

The Bible quotes Jesus as saying, "I am come to set a man at variance against his father, and the daughter against her mother, and the daughter in law against her mother in law. And a man's foes shall be they of his own household" (Matthew 10:35-36). This is a quote from Micah 7:6, "For the son dishonoureth the father, the daughter riseth up against her mother, the daughter in law against her mother in law; a man's enemies [oyeb] are the men of his own house".

Many other sayings of Jesus reinforce this concept. "Brother shall deliver up the brother to death, and the father the child: and the children shall rise up against their parents, and cause them to be put to death. And ye shall be hated of all men for my name's sake" (Matthew 10:21-22). "They shall lay their hands on you, and persecute you, delivering you up to the synagogues, and into prisons, being brought before kings and rulers for my name's sake" (Luke 21:12, see also Mark 13:9). "I send you forth as sheep in the midst of wolves ... But beware of men: for they will deliver you up to the councils, and they will scourge you in their synagogues" (Matthew 10:16-17). "Wherefore, behold, I send unto you prophets, and wise men, and scribes: and some of them ye shall kill and crucify; and some of them shall ye scourge in your synagogues, and persecute them from city to city: That upon you may come all the righteous blood shed upon the earth, from the blood of righteous Abel unto the blood of Zacharias son of Barachias, whom ye slew between the temple and the altar" (Matthew 23:34-35). "Blessed are they which are persecuted for righteousness' sake: for theirs is the kingdom of heaven. Blessed are ye, when men shall revile you, and persecute you, and shall say all manner of evil against you falsely, for my sake. Rejoice, and be exceeding glad: for great is your reward in heaven: for so persecuted they the prophets which were before you" (Matthew 5:10-12).

The Apostle Paul said, "all that will live godly in Christ Jesus shall suffer persecution" (2 Timothy 3:12). He should know, "Of the Jews five times received I forty stripes save one, thrice was I beaten with rods, once was I stoned" (2 Corinthians 11:24-25).

The Bible claims that God was very pleased with Jesus (Matthew 3:17, 17:5) and that Jesus was sinless (1 Peter 1:19). Despite the prediction of Proverbs 16:7, Jesus' enemies were certainly not at peace with him. They tried to kill him when he was less than two years old (Matthew 2:13-18).

They called him Beelzebub Prince of Devils (Matthew12:24, 9:34, 10:25, Mark 3:22, Luke 11:15). They tried to push him off a cliff (Luke 4:29-30). The Bible also says that they scourged Jesus, mocked him, put a crown of thorns on his head, and crucified him.

False Prophecy #12

In Matthew 18:19-20, Jesus predicted, "I say unto you, if two of you shall agree on earth as touching any thing that they shall ask, it shall be done for them of my Father which is in heaven. For where two or three are gathered in my name, there I am in the midst of them". Psalm 103:2-3 says, "Bless the Lord ... who healeth all thy diseases". If these verses were really true, ambulances would not need paramedics and hospitals would not need doctors or medicines. All they would need would be two or three little old ladies who were right with Jesus, agreed with each other and liked to pray.

If Matthew 18:19-20 is true, why do nonreligious hospitals cure people just as well as hospitals that are sponsored by Catholics, Presbyterians, etc.? Why do some nations with few Bible believers, such as Japan, have longevity rates that are better than the United States, which has a large percentage of Bible believers? Why has human longevity increased dramatically over the past 150 years while the percentage of Bible believers has decreased just as dramatically over the same time period? *Why does penicillin without prayer work better than prayer without penicillin?*

Biblical literalists try to wiggle out of this one by saying that Jesus always answers prayers, but sometimes Jesus' answer is not "yes"; it is "wait", "something different" or "no". There are two fatal flaws with this argument.

First, that is nowhere close to what the Bible says. The Bible says that Jesus explicitly said, "it shall be done for them", not "something different", not "no", and if their prayer needs a quick response (like when Granny has a heart attack), not "wait".

Second, no matter who/what you ask for something, whether it is Jesus, Mithra, Zeus, your deceased ancestors or no one at all, one of those four things has to happen because those four things include all possibilities. Either you will get what you asked for, you will get something different from what you asked for, you will get what you asked for later than you asked for it, or you will not get anything at all.

The Bible describes several situations where groups of sincere followers of Jehovah/Jesus people prayed unselfishly and did not get what they prayed for. For example, see 2 Kings 15:3-5 and Exodus 2:23-24.

False Prophecy #13

In Matthew 19:28, Jesus told his disciples "ye also shall sit upon twelve thrones, judging the twelve tribes of Israel". Yet we are told later that Judas Iscariot betrayed Jesus and "it had been good for that man if he had not been born" (Matthew 26:24). Not even the most ardent Biblical literalist believes that Judas Iscariot will be on one of those thrones.

False Prophecy #14

Mark 8:31 says, "He [Jesus] began to teach them, that the Son of man must suffer many things, and be rejected of the elders, and of the chief priests, and scribes, and be killed, and after three days rise again". The ancient Greek manuscripts clearly and consistently say "<u>after</u> three days", which is why this phrase in this verse is translated "after three days" in the KJB, NASB, RSB, NIB and JB.

But other Bible passages repeatedly and definitely say that Jesus died on Friday afternoon and was raised around dawn on Sunday morning. That is not "after three days"; it is barely a day and a half. Even if you counted Friday afternoon as a full day, the earliest you could get "after three days" would be Sunday evening.

Other Bible verses make a different prediction. John 2:19-21 says, "Jesus answered and said unto them, Destroy this temple, and in three days I will raise it up ... But he spake of the temple of his body". (See also Matthew 16:21, 17:23, 20:19, Mark 9:31, Luke 9:22, 13:32, 18:33, 24:7 and Acts 10:40.) All of these verses contradict Mark 8:31, because they all say that Jesus would rise "in three days" or simply "the third day" (many modern translations say "on the third day" in these verses). But Mark 8:31 clearly says "<u>after three days</u>".

False Prophecy #15

In Matthew 25:41, Jesus predicted, "Then shall he say also unto them on the left hand, Depart from me, ye cursed, into everlasting fire, prepared for the devil and his angels." Matthew 25:46 says, "these shall go away into everlasting punishment." See also Jeremiah 17:4, Malachi 1:4 and Revelation 20:1-15.

But Micah 7:18 says, "he [God] retaineth not his anger for ever". Psalm 30:5 says, "his anger endureth but a moment". Jeremiah 3:12 says, "I am merciful, saith the Lord, and I will not keep anger for ever".

False Prophecy #16

In Matthew 26:29, Jesus said, "I say unto you, I will not drink henceforth of this fruit of the vine, until that day when I drink it new with you in my Father's kingdom" (see also Mark 14:25). This was at the Last Supper, before Jesus was crucified.

But John 19:28-30 says that while he was on the cross "Jesus knowing that all things were now accomplished, that the scripture might be fulfilled, saith, 'I thirst'. Now there was set a vessel full of vinegar [sour wine] and they filled a sponge with vinegar, and put it upon hyssop, and put it to his mouth. When Jesus therefore had received the vinegar, he said, 'It is finished.'"

Jesus did not merely taste the sour wine. The Bible says that he drank it. The Greek word translated "received" in John 19:30 is "lambano". Lambano means much more than just "taste" or "touch". It is the same word used in Acts 9:19 "when he had received [lambano] meat, he was strengthened" and 2 Corinthians 11:24 "five times I received [lambano] forty lashes save one." "Lambano" is used in numerous verses to indicate that someone receives completely, such as John 1:12 "As many as received [lambano] him, to them gave he power to become the sons of God", John 20:22, "Receive [lambano] ye the Holy Ghost" and Romans 1:4-5 "The Son of God ... by whom we have receive [lambano] grace and apostleship".

False Prophecy #17

Matthew 26:34 says, "Jesus said unto him [Peter], Verily I say unto thee, That this night, before the cock crow, thou shalt deny me thrice". A few verses later, Matthew 26:70-75 claims that this "prophecy" was "fulfilled" after Peter's third denial. But Mark 14:66-72 clearly says that a cock crowed after Peter's first denial – before his second and third denial.

False Prophecy #18

Mark 16:17-18 predicts "these signs shall follow them that believe ... if they drink any deadly thing, it shall not harm them." This book will not discuss the Bible believers who deliberately drink strychnine or other poisons to test their faith, because they are a dying breed (literally). There are more serious problems with this prophecy.

Mark 16:17-18's prophecy is false for all Christians. It is simply not true that Christians' response to poisons is different from anyone else's. Many oral medications, such as narcotics, are available in liquid form for patients who cannot swallow pills. These liquid medications have exactly the same label for Christians as for non-Christians: take it precisely as your doctor tells you to. Take too much of it and it will harm you and might even kill you.

A much more common "deadly thing" that people drink is polluted water. Again, there is precisely zero evidence that Christians respond to polluted water any differently from anyone else. In the early 21st century, in Anniston, Alabama, a very strongly Christian conservative area of the United States, it was proven in court that dioxin contamination of the water supply caused cancers in thousands of people[4]. No one dared to argue that this was impossible or even unlikely because thousands of these people were Christians.

In most of the world, the most common form of water pollution is by pathogenic (disease causing) viruses and bacteria. This kills millions of people every year even in modern times. In medieval times, when just about all of Europe was Christian, polluted water was a major reason why the lifespan was only about one-third of what it is today.

If Mark 16:17-18 is true, we should be able to go into Nigeria, Bangladesh or other areas with bad water and dramatically reduce the rates of cholera, diphtheria and childhood/infant diarrhea by getting people to become Christians, because "if they drink any deadly thing, it shall not harm them". This is absurd, of course, because whatever your personal beliefs may be, you are going to get just as sick as any other saint or sinner if you drink water polluted with coliform bacteria, amoebas, typhoid germs, dioxin, arsenic, lead, etc.

False Prophecy #19

Matthew 27:57-60 says that Jesus was buried in a sepulcher belonging to Joseph of Arimathea, "a rich man" (Matthew 27:57). Many apologists and commentators[5] claim that this is a fulfillment of a prophecy in Isaiah 53:9, "he made his grave with the wicked, and with the rich in his death".

But the Bible also says that Joseph of Arimathea "himself was Jesus' disciple" (Matthew 27:57), "an honorable counselor, which also waited for the Kingdom of God" (Mark 15:43), "a good man, and just ... who also himself waited for the kingdom of God" (Luke 23:50-51) and "a disciple of Jesus" (John 19:38). Clearly, the Bible repeatedly says that Joseph of Arimathea was not "wicked".

Also, the Bible says that this sepulcher was "his [Joseph's] own new tomb" (Matthew 27:60), "wherein never man before was laid" (Luke 23:53), "a new sepulcher, wherein was never man yet laid" (John 19:41). So not only did Jesus not make "his grave with the wicked", he didn't make his grave with anyone!

The resurrection of Jesus, if it occurred, was arguably the most important event in human history. But no one knows where or when it happened. Modern New Testament believers claim two possible places. Catholics have built The Church of the Holy Sepulcher over one place. Many Protestants believe that Jesus' tomb was actually a place now called The Garden Tomb.

Not only do Christians disagree about where the resurrection happened, they disagree about when it happened. Easter for the Greek Orthodox church is usually celebrated on a different date from the Easter celebrated by Catholics and Protestants.

These disputes constitute powerful evidence against the historicity of Jesus' resurrection: believers cannot agree among themselves about the place and time of the one event which is the basis for all of their faith (1 Corinthians 15:17-19).

False Prophecy #20

In Luke 1:32, an angel said, "the Lord God shall give unto him [Jesus] the throne of his father David". But Matthew 1:11-12 lists Jeconiah as one of Jesus' ancestors and the Bible clearly says that no descendant of Jechoniah will sit on the throne of David.

"Josias begat Jechonias and his brethren, about the time they were carried away to Babylon, And after they were brought to Babylon, Jechonias begat Salathiel" (see also 1 Chronicles 3:17-18). Jeremiah 22:30 prophesies, "Thus saith the Lord, Write ye this man [Judah's king Jeconiah, see 22:24 and 22:28] childless, a man that shall not prosper in his days: for no man of his seed shall prosper, sitting upon the throne of David, and ruling any more in Judah".

False Prophecy #21

Luke 8:10 says, "And he [Jesus] said, Unto you [the disciples] it is given to know the mysteries of the kingdom of God: but to others in parables; that seeing they might not see, and hearing they might not understand". Jesus was claming to have fulfilled the "prophecy" in Isaiah 6:9-10, where God commanded Isaiah, "Go, and tell this people, Hear ye indeed, but understand not; and see ye indeed, but perceive not. Make the heart of this people fat, and make their ears heavy, and shut their eyes; lest they see with their eyes, and hear with their ears, and understand with their heart, and convert, and be healed". God commanded Isaiah to do this "Until the cities be wasted without inhabitant, and the houses without man, and the land be utterly desolate" (Isaiah 6:11).

What reason could Jesus possibly have to not wanting everyone to understand that the mysteries of the kingdom of God? It is difficult to imagine a more emphatic contradiction with Jesus own words, "it is not the will of your Father which is in heaven, that one of these little ones should perish" (Matthew 18:14), Jesus parable of the lost sheep (Luke 15:1-10), Jesus statement "there is joy in the presence of the angels of God over one sinner that repenteth" (Luke 15:10) Jesus claim that "For the Son of man is come to seek and to save that which was lost" (Luke 19:10), or the Apostle Peter's claim, "The Lord is not slack concerning his promise, as some men count slackness; but is longsuffering to us-ward, not willing that any should perish, but that all should come to repentance" (2 Peter 3:9).

False Prophecy #22

In Luke 23:43, Jesus said to one of the thieves who were crucified with him, "Verily I say unto thee, To day shalt thou be with me in paradise." Although the thief might have gone to paradise that day, the Bible clearly says that Jesus did not go to paradise until at least two days later.

Before his crucifixion, Jesus said, "as Jonas was three days and three nights in the whale's belly, so shall the Son of Man be three days and three nights in the heart of the earth" (Matthew 12:39-40). On the Sunday morning of his resurrection, Jesus told Mary Magdalene, "Touch me not; for I am not yet ascended to my Father" (John 20:17).

False Prophecy #23

In John 7:38, Jesus predicted fulfillment of an alleged Old Testament prophecy, "He that believeth on me, as the scripture hath said, out of his belly shall flow rivers of living water". There is nothing in the Old Testament that says anything close to "out of his belly shall flow rivers of living water".

The Greek word translated "scripture" in John 7:38 is "graphe". 2 Timothy 3:16 says, "All scripture [graphe] is given by inspiration of God, and is profitable for doctrine, for reproof, for correction, for instruction in righteousness". But in this verse, Jesus himself clearly called something

17

"scripture" that is nowhere in the 39 books of the Old Testament. This is not just a false prophecy, this is a fraudulent prophecy because it claims that the Old Testament says something that it does not say.

False Prophecy #24

Ezekiel 26:7-12 prophesies,

"For thus saith the Lord God; Behold, I will bring upon Tyrus Nebuchadrezzar king of Babylon, a king of kings, from the north, with horses, and with chariots, and with horsemen, and companies, and much people. He shall slay with the sword thy daughters in the field: and he shall make a fort against thee, and cast a mount against thee, and lift up the buckler against thee. And he shall set engines of war against thy walls, and with his axes he shall break down thy towers. By reason of the abundance of his horses their dust shall cover thee: thy walls shall shake at the noise of the horsemen, and of the wheels, and of the chariots, when he shall enter into thy gates, as men enter into a city wherein is made a breach. With the hoofs of his horses shall he tread down all thy streets: he shall slay thy people by the sword, and thy strong garrisons shall go down to the ground. And they shall make a spoil of thy riches, and make a prey of thy merchandise: and they shall break down thy walls, and destroy thy pleasant houses: and they shall lay thy stones and thy timber and thy dust in the midst of the water."

This prophecy did <u>not</u> come true. Nebuchadrezzar beseiged Tyrus (Tyre) for 13 years from 586-573 BCE, but was unable to conquer it. Ezekiel 29:18-20 confirms that Nebuchadrezzar was unable to conquer Tyre, and even claims that God gave him Egypt instead "because they wrought for me"(see Jeremiah 25:9, 27:6-8, 43:10). "Nebuchadrezzar king of Babylon caused his army to serve a great service against Tyrus: every head was made bald, and every shoulder was peeled: yet had he no wages, nor his army, for Tyrus, for the service that he had served against it: Therefore thus saith the Lord God; Behold, I will give the land of Egypt unto Nebuchadrezzar king of Babylon; and he shall take her multitude, and take her spoil, and take her prey; and it shall be the wages for his army. I have given him the land of Egypt for his labour wherewith he served against it, because they wrought for me, saith the Lord God."

In Ezekiel chapters 26-28, God waxed eloquent with many prophecies that the city of Tyrus would be destroyed, never again inhabited or rebuilt, and covered by water. "I will make thee like the top of a rock: thou shalt be a place to spread nets upon; thou shalt be built no more: for I the

18

Lord have spoken it, saith the Lord God" (Ezekiel 26:14, see also 26:4). "Thus saith the Lord God; When I shall make thee a desolate city, like the cities that are not inhabited; when I shall bring up the deep upon thee, and great waters shall cover thee. When I shall bring thee down with them that descend into the pit, with the people of old time, and shall set thee in the low parts of the earth, in places desolate of old, with them that go down to the pit, that thou be not inhabited; and I shall set glory in the land of the living, I will make thee a terror, and thou shalt be no more: though thou be sought for, yet shalt thou never be found again, saith the Lord God" (Ezekiel 26:19-21). "Thou shalt be a terror, and never shalt be any more" (Ezekiel 27:36).

These are some of the most specific and clear prophecies in the Bible. They are also completely wrong. Despite being frequently conquered like most Middle Eastern cities, Tyre (Tyrus) continued to be populated through New Testament times (Matthew 15:21, Mark 3:8, 7:24, 7:31, Luke 6:17, Acts 12:20, 21:3, 21:7) and afterwards to the present. Today, Tyre has over 100,000 inhabitants and is the fourth largest city in Lebanon.

False Prophecy #25

In John 14:12 Jesus said, "Verily, verily, I say unto you, He that believeth on me, the works that I do shall he do also; and greater works than these shall he do, because I go unto my Father". But other passages in the Bible say that Jesus did at least four things that no Christian has ever come close to accomplishing.

(1) From a Christian point of view, it is difficult to imagine a "greater work" than Jesus dying for the sins of humanity. By definition, no other human being can do that because all other humans are sinners.

(2) The one thing that could be "greater" than Jesus dying for people's sins is his Resurrection. According to Christian theology, the Resurrection was different from, and much better than, other "raisings from the dead" performed by Jesus' Apostles (Acts 20:9-12), because those people whom the Apostles raised eventually physically died again, but Jesus did not die again.

(3) The Bible says that Jesus has abolished death (2 Timothy 1:10).

(4) Jesus was God (John 1:1, 10:30), so Jesus created the Universe (Genesis chapters 1-2).

False Prophecy #26

In John 14:13-14, Jesus predicted, "And whatsoever ye shall ask in my name, that will I do, that the Father may be glorified in the Son. If ye shall ask any thing in my name, I will do it" (see also John 15:7 and 15:16). This is about as specific a promise as you can get, from an omnipotent (all-powerful) deity who can do just about anything. It is also demonstrably bogus. Jesus' followers devote enormous effort to rationalizing why God does not do what they ask in reasonable, faithful, unselfish prayers. See also comments on False Prophecy #12.

It is beyond the scope of this book to detail the trillions of unanswered prayers that have been faithfully prayed by sincere Bible believers. Here are just two examples whose non-answers can be objectively verified. **#1**: The Southeastern United States is the very heart of the "Bible Belt", with a greater percentage of conservative Bible Believers than any major region in the world. But the Bible Belt trails behind the rest of the United States and non-Christian nations such as Japan in quality of life measures such as longevity and infant mortality, even though Christian children pray for the health of their parents and Christian parents pray for the health of their children.

#2: Jesus prayed that his followers would be "one" (John 17:11) and repeatedly promised that the Holy Spirit would guide believers to the truth (see John 14:26, 15:26 and 16:13-15). This has obviously not happened. The church is split up into literally thousands of denominations, each one thoroughly convinced that the beliefs they received from the Bible and the Holy Spirit are the most completely correct ones. There is just one Holy Spirit. If the Holy Spirit told different things about key doctrines to different groups of believers, he would be lying to at least all but one of those groups.

Even in the Bible, God did not answer heartfelt, unselfish prayers from a sincere, repentant believer, even when those prayers were asking God to fulfill God's own promise and law. 2 Samuel 11-12 tells the story of David and Bathsheba, when David committed adultery with Bathsheba and murdered her husband Uriah. Then the prophet Nathan told David, "Because by this deed thou hast given great occasion to the enemies of the Lord to blaspheme, the child also that is born unto thee shall surely die" (2 Samuel 12:14). David confessed his sin (2 Samuel 12:13, see also 1 John 1:9), but "the Lord struck the child that Uriah's wife bare unto David, and it was very sick. David therefore besought God for the child; and David fasted, and went in, and lay all night upon the earth. And the elders of his house arose, and went to him, to raise him up from the earth: but he would not, neither did he eat bread with them" (2 Samuel 12:15-17, see also 12:22). David had every reason to believe that God would spare his son, because Old Testament Law said, "The fathers shall not be put to death for the children, neither shall the children be put to death for the fathers, every man shall be put to death for his own sin" (Deuteronomy 24:16). For God to kill David's child because of David's sin would break God's own law and promise. But "it came to pass on the seventh day, that the child died" (2 Samuel 12:18).

For another unanswered prayer, see 2 Corinthians 12:7-9.

False Prophecy #27

John 15:25 says, "But this cometh to pass, that the word might be fulfilled that is written in their law, They hated me without a cause". What is supposedly being "fulfilled" in this verse is a misquote of either Psalm 69:4 or Psalm 35:19, neither of which actually predict anything.

Psalm 69:4 says, "They that hate me without a cause are more than the hairs of mine head". But Psalm 69 cannot possibly be talking about Christ. The very next verse says, "O God, thou knowest my foolishness; and my sins are not hid from thee" (Psalm 69:5). The Bible teaches that Jesus did not have any sins and that he was not foolish. Psalm 69:13 says, "in the multitude of thy mercy hear me" (see also Psalm 69:16). Jesus did not need God's mercy. If Jesus had needed God's mercy, he could not have been the sacrifice for anyone else's sins. Psalm 69:18 asks that God "redeem" the Psalmist's soul. If Jesus' soul needed redeeming, he could not have redeemed anyone else's soul.

Psalm 35:19 says, "Let not them that are mine enemies wrongfully rejoice over me: neither let them wink with the eye that hate me without a cause". Nowhere in this Psalm does it claim to be talking about the Messiah. If this verse is a "prophecy", it has the least predictive value of any prophecy ever made. Just about every human being who has ever lived has, at some time in his/her life, been hated by some other people for no good reason. This would apply even to animals who have raised the ire of some humans without there being any basis for the hatred. There is nothing unique or even unusual about someone or something being hated without cause.

False Prophecy #28

In John 16:13-15, Jesus predicted, "Howbeit when he, the Spirit of truth, is come, he will guide you into all truth: for he shall not speak of himself; but whatsoever he shall hear, that shall he speak: and he will shew you things to come. He shall glorify me: for he shall receive of mine, and shall shew it unto you. All things that the Father hath are mine: therefore said I, that he shall take of mine, and shall shew it unto you". (See also John 14:26 and 15:26.)

This is one of the most demonstrably false passages in the Bible. The evidence for this is very clear and provided by Bible believers themselves. The same evidence also strongly supports the idea that the Bible does contradict itself on major doctrines.

Look in the phone book of any major city which has a large Christian population. You will see listings for dozens if not hundreds of different Christian denominations. There are Catholics, Presbyterians, Baptists, Pentecostals, Seventh Day Adventists, etc. Most of these have further split into smaller, but still completely separate, denominations such as Cumberland Presbyterian, Presbyterian Church USA, Reformed Presbyterian, Reformed Presbyterian Evangelical Synod, Presbyterian Church America, Southern Baptist, Primitive Baptist, Missionary Baptist, American Baptist, Freewill Baptist, Reformed Baptist, National Baptist, Seventh Day Baptist, General Conference Baptist, General Association of Regular Baptist, etc.

If the Holy Spirit is "guiding into all truth" all of these devoted born again Bible believers who are collectively spending billions of hours studying the Bible and sincerely praying that God will help them interpret it correctly, have confessed their sins and believe that they are in constant communication with God (1 Thessalonians 5:17), then why do the thousands of denominations disagree on major Bible doctrines so strongly that they have to break off and create their own denomination?

Jesus himself prayed for unity among believers (John 17:21-23). The Bible condemns such divisiveness (1 Corinthians 1:10-17, Ephesians 4:3-6), so believers are sinning (1 Corinthians 3:3-7) as well as committing heresy (1 Corinthians 11:18-19) unless they are members of the one only truly correct denomination. The problem is that the Holy Spirit is not telling which denomination is the only truly correct one. Or more precisely, the Holy Spirit is telling every denomination that their own denomination is the only truly correct one!

False Prophecy #29

Acts 1:16-20 says, "Men and brethren, this scripture must needs have been fulfilled, which the Holy Ghost by the mouth of David spake before concerning Judas, which was guide to them that took Jesus. For he

22

[Judas Iscariot] was numbered with us, and had obtained part of this ministry. Now this man purchased a field with the reward of iniquity; and falling headlong, he burst asunder in the midst, and all his bowels gushed out. And it was known unto all the dwellers at Jerusalem; insomuch as that field is called in their proper tongue, Aceldama, that is to say, The field of blood. For it is written in the book of Psalms, Let his habitation be desolate, and let no man dwell therein: and his bishoprick let another take"

This is supposedly a fulfillment of an alleged Messianic Prophecy in Psalm 69:25, "Let their habitation be desolate; and let none dwell in their tents". The problem is that the speaker in Psalm 69 cannot possibly be Christ. Psalm 69:5 says, "O God, thou knowest my foolishness; and my sins are not hid from thee". The Bible teaches that Jesus was the exact opposite of foolish or sinful. Psalm 69:13 says, "O God, in the multitude of thy mercy hear me" and Psalm 69:16 says, "Turn unto me according to the multitude of thy tender mercies". If Jesus needed mercy, he could not have paid the price for anyone's sins. Psalm 69:18 says, "Draw nigh unto my soul, and redeem it". If Jesus' soul needed redemption, he could not have redeemed anyone else.

"Let his bishoprick let another take" is a quote from Psalm 109:8. As with Psalm 69, the speaker in Psalm 109 cannot possibly be Christ. Psalm 109:26 says, "O Lord my God, O save me according to thy mercy".

False Prophecy #30

Acts 2:25-27 quotes Psalm 16:10 as a Messianic prophecy, "For David speaketh concerning him [Jesus] ... For thou wilt not leave my soul in hell; neither wilt thou suffer thine Holy One to see corruption" (see also Acts 13:35). This interpretation of Psalm 16:10 takes this verse badly out of context. Other verses in Psalm 16 make it very clear that Psalm 16:10 cannot be talking about Christ.

Psalm 16:1 says, "Preserve me, O God". But Jesus is co-equal with God and is therefore omnipotent, so he does not need preserving. He can take care of himself.

Psalm 16:2 says, "O my soul, thou hast said unto the Lord, Thou art my Lord: my goodness extendeth not to thee". The last phrase is more clear in the Revised Standard Bible (RSB), "I have no good apart from Thee". If this verse is a Messianic Prophecy, it calls into question the whole idea of the atonement, i.e., the idea that Jesus was a perfect sacrifice for the sins of all humanity (Hebrews 9:14, 1 Peter 1:19). On the cross, Jesus was separated from God (Matthew 27:46, Mark 15:34). So if Jesus had no good

23

when separated from God, he could not have been a sacrifice for our sins.

Psalm 16:8 says, "I have set the Lord always before me: because he is at my right hand, I shall not be moved" (see also verse 11). But Jesus is on God's right hand, which means that God the Father is on Jesus' left hand (Luke 20:42-43, see also Psalm 110:1).

Psalm 16:11 says, "Thou wilt shew me the path of life". But Jesus is co-equal with God (John 14:7), and is therefore omniscient. He already knows "the path of life". In fact, Jesus is "the life" (John 14:6).

False Prophecy #31

Acts 2:30 says, "Therefore [King David] being a prophet, and knowing that God had sworn with an oath to him, that of the fruit of his loins, according to the flesh, he would raise up Christ to sit on his throne" (see also Romans 1:3).

But Matthew and Luke both trace Jesus' genealogy from David through Joseph (Matthew 1:16, Luke 3:23). The Bible is very clear that there was not one atom of Joseph's biological heredity ("the fruit of his loins according to the flesh") in Jesus, because Jesus was conceived by the Holy Spirit (Matthew 1:20 see also Matthew 1:18-25 and Luke 1:34-35).

False Prophecy #32

Acts 8:32 says, "The place of the scripture which he read was this, He was led as a sheep to the slaughter; and like a lamb dumb before his shearer, so opened he not his mouth". This verse is referring to Isaiah 53:7, which says, "He was oppressed, and he was afflicted, yet he opened not his mouth: he is brought as a lamb to the slaughter, and as a sheep before her shearers is dumb, so he openeth not his mouth".

This is supposedly a Messianic Prophecy. If so, it is a false prophecy, because the Bible says that Jesus did in fact speak at least 15 times during his trial and crucifixion:
- John 18:20-21 - Jesus spoke to the high priest
- John 18:23 - Jesus spoke to the high priest
- Matthew 26:64, Mark 14:62, Luke 22:67-69 - "Thou hast said: nevertheless I say unto you, Hereafter shall ye see the Son of man sitting on the right hand of power, and coming in the clouds of heaven".
- Luke 22:70 - "thou sayest I am" in front of the Sanhedrin
- John 18:34 - "sayest thou this thing yourself" to Pilate
- John 18:36 - "my kingdom is not of this world" to Pilate

- Matthew 27:11, Mark 15:2, Luke 23:3, John 18:37 - "Art thou the King of the Jews? And Jesus said unto him, Thou sayest" to Pilate
  - John 19:11 - "thou couldest have no power against me except it were given thee" to Pilate
  - Luke 23:28-31 - Jesus spoke to the daughters of Jerusalem
  - John 19:26-27 - "woman behold thy son"
  - Luke 23:34 - "father forgive them"
  - Luke 23:43 - "Verily I say unto thee, To day shalt thou be with me in paradise"
  - Matthew 27:46, Mark 15:34 - "Eli, Eli, lama sabachthani"
  - John 19:30 - "it is finished"
  - Matthew 27:50, Mark 15:37, Luke 23:46 - "when he had cried again with a loud voice, yielded up the ghost"

False Prophecy #33

Romans 2:5-6 predicts, "…the righteous judgment of God, who will render to every man according to his deeds". But the Bible contains several clear examples of God punishing other people for the sins of his "chosen", while not punishing his "chosen" at all for those same sins.

2 Samuel 24:1-25 says that David sinned and that, as punishment, God sent a plague on Israel that killed 70,000 people in three days and left David unharmed. In the famous case of David and Bathsheba, God punished other people, not David (see 2 Samuel 11:1-12:24). Abram deceived Pharaoh, so God sent a plague on Egypt, not on Abram (Genesis 12:10-20). Abraham and Sarah deceived Abimelech, king of Gerar, and God "fast closed up all of the wombs of the house of Abimelech" (Genesis 20:1-18), but Abraham actually became wealthier.

The Bible also provides many examples of God not punishing some of the most egregious sins. God did not punish King David when he sexually mutilated 200 corpses (1 Samuel 18:20-27), committed genocide on the Geshurites, Gezrites, and Amalekites (1 Samuel 27:8-12), Moabites (2 Samuel 8:2) and Edomites (1 Kings 11:15-16) and ordered the slaughter of people with disabilities (2 Samuel 5:7-10). God did not punish Solomon when he ordered his hit man to assassinate a political enemy (1 Kings 2:13-25). The Israelites murdered almost the entire Israelite tribe of Benjamin and God did not punish them at all (Judges Chapter 21). God let Samson get away with murder (Judges 14:11-20).

The Bible also provides examples of some people being severely punished for a sin, and other people who committed the exact same sin not being punished at all. God ordered the execution of 3,000 Israelites who worshipped the Golden Calf; but Aaron, who made the calf, built an altar for it and told the Israelites to worship it, was not punished at all (Exodus 32:4-5, 32:35), even though this was a capital offense according to Exodus 20:3-5 and Deuteronomy 13:6-10. Aaron was even allowed to continue serving as high priest. Moses' brother Aaron and sister Miriam both spoke against Moses in the same verses for the same reasons, but God struck only Miriam with leprosy (Numbers 12:1-15).

Genocide is probably the most extreme sin that any human can commit. But God did not punish the Israelites at all for the genocidal extermination of the people living in Palestine when the Israelites invaded during Moses' and Joshua's lifetimes. God not only did not punish the Israelites for these mass murders, he commanded the Israelites to commit them. It was not a sin to kill all of those women and children, it was a sin not to. (See Deuteronomy 20:16-18 and Joshua chapters 10-11).

False Prophecy #34

2 Thessalonians 2:3 predicts, "Let no man deceive you by any means: for that day [the glorious return of Jesus] shall not come, except there come a falling away first". Many Christian fundamentalist preachers act as though this was some wonderful prediction which is only just now coming true in our lifetimes. Each generation of Bible believers has been led to believe that theirs is the last because Jesus' return is imminent. When this author was in college, a para-church group attempted to recruit me to work for them as full-time paid staff. I planned to go to graduate school, but they told me that they were sure that Jesus would return so soon that I would not have time to complete my degree in graduate school. Much to their dismay, I went to graduate school instead of working for them. It's a good thing that I did, because that was in 1977 and we are still waiting. See also False Prophecy #100.

One of the "proofs" that these are the "last days" (2 Peter 3:3-4) is the "falling away" predicted in 2 Thessalonians 2:3. But this "prediction" has come true hundreds of times since the first century. From New Testament times (1 Corinthians 1:10-17, Revelation 3:14-18) through Constantine through Luther through the present day, Christianity has been fraught with one schism after another, one heresy after another, in an endless cycle of "falling aways" followed by an equally endless cycle of "reforms", "awakenings" and "revivals", in what are now thousands of different

Christian denominations, many of which believe that most other denominations are in constant states of unrepentant apostasy/heresy.

For example, Protestant theologian Matthew Henry, writing his commentary on 2 Thessalonians Chapter 2 in the early 1700's, provided detailed arguments describing why the Catholic church was the "falling away" and the Pope was the "man of sin". Of course, if this was true, then it had been true for over 1,000 years at the time that Henry was writing, and could hardly be considered a sign that Jesus' return was soon to take place.

This is not a uniquely New Testament phenomenon. The Old Testament reports one apostasy after another, then time and again God's chosen got back on the narrow way. A prediction which predicts something that happens every day needs no divine insprer to make it come true; it only needs a shrewd predictor.

False Prophecy #35

Hebrews 1:5 claims that Jesus fulfilled a the prediction of a passage in the Old Testament, "For unto which of the angels said he at any time ... I will be to him a Father, and he shall be to me a Son?". This is a reference to one of two Old Testament passages, neither of which can possibly refer to Jesus.

One of these passages is 1 Chronicles 17:12-13, where God spoke to David concerning his son, "He shall build me a house, and I will stablish his throne for ever. I will be his father, and he shall be my son: and I will not take my mercy away from him". This obviously cannot refer to Jesus, because Jesus never needed God's mercy, so the statement that God would not "take away my mercy" from Jesus is nonsense. If Jesus had needed God's mercy, he could not have been the atonement for anyone else's sins. Also, it is an essential part of Christian belief that Jesus is God, that he is part of the Trinity. The possibility of God taking away mercy from himself is absurd.

The other passage is 2 Samuel 7:13-15, which refers to a similar (possibly the same) communication from God to David. "He shall build an house for my name, and I will stablish the throne of his kingdom for ever. I will be his father, and he shall be my son. If he commit iniquity, I will chasten him with the rod of men, and with the stripes of the children of men, But my mercy shall not depart away from him". Not only does this passage contain the same problematic reference to God not taking away his mercy from this person, it goes on to say that God will chasten him "if he commit iniquity". This would be nonsense if it was referring to sinless Jesus, but makes a lot of sense if it referred to the sinful kings of Judah and Israel who were descended from David

False Prophecy #36

Hebrews 10:7 says, "Then said I, Lo, I come (in the volume of the book it is written of me,) to do thy will, O God". This is universally regarded by New Testament believers as a fulfilled Messianic prophecy because this is a direct quote from Psalm 40:7.

But other verses in Psalm 40 clearly say that this Psalm cannot be referring to a sinless person. Psalm 40:11 says, "withhold not thy tender mercies from me, O Lord". Psalm 40:12 says, "mine iniquities have taken hold upon me". Since Jesus did not need God's mercy, nor did he have any iniquity, Psalm 40 is referring to someone who had sinned, not Jesus

False Prophecy #37

In Genesis 13:15, God told Abraham, "For all the land which thou seest, to thee will I give it, and to thy seed for ever". In Genesis 13:17 God told Abraham, "Arise, walk through the land in the length of it and in the breadth of it; for I will give it unto thee". God repeated this promise to Abraham in Genesis 17:8 and to Jacob in Genesis 28:13.

God made a point of telling Abraham that he himself would receive the promised land. Note that God promised it to both Abraham and his seed (descendants), not just his seed. But Acts 7:5 and Hebrews 11:13 says that Abraham did not receive it, only his descendants did, over 500 years later. That is like promising a Christopher Columbus in 1492 that you were going to give him the United States, but not doing so until five centuries later, in 1992.

In Genesis 17:8, God told Abraham "And I will give unto thee, and to thy seed after thee, the land wherein thou art a stranger, all the land of Canaan, for an everlasting possession". But Acts 7:5 says, that God "gave him [Abraham] none of the inheritance in it, no, not so much as to set his foot on", and Hebrews 11:13 says that Abraham , "died in faith, not having received the promises". Abraham did not receive the promised land, only his descendants did, over 500 years later.

Apologists claim that this promise was fulfilled because Abraham's descendants ("seed") did eventually receive the Promised Land. But Genesis 17:8 clearly says not just Abraham's descendants would receive the Promised Land, Abraham himself would receive it: "I will give unto thee, and to thy seed after thee".

Apologists argue that giving the land to Jacob and giving it to his descendants was the same thing, because Jacob's descendants were inside his "loins" according to Biblical beliefs. For example, in Genesis 35:11, God promised Jacob, "kings shall come out of thy loins". Hebrews 7:9-10 claims that Abraham's great-grandson "Levi ... payed tithes in Abraham, for he was yet in the loins of his father". Acts 2:29-30 says "David ... God had sworn with an oath to him, that of the fruit of his loins, according to the flesh, he would raise up Christ to sit on his throne"; this would happen either 28 generations later (Matthew 1:6-17) or 42 generations later (Luke 3:23-31).

This idea is genetically absurd. Any six year old child who reads a book about "where babies come from" knows more about modern genetics than the writers of the above verses.

Believers in the book of Genesis are seldom persuaded by over-whelming scientific evidence, however, so it should also be pointed out that this "explanation" disagrees with the obvious statement of the text, which clearly makes a distinction between Abraham and his "seed" by naming them separately and saying that God will give the land to Abraham and his seed. The Bible makes the same distinction with Jacob.

False Prophecy #38

2 Peter 3:3-4 says, "Knowing this first, that there shall come in the last days scoffers, walking after their own lusts, And saying, Where is the promise of his coming? for since the fathers fell asleep, all things continue as they were from the beginning of the creation". Christian conservatives often quote these verses as a "prophecy" that "proves" that these are the last days and Jesus is coming back any minute.

This is not a prophecy; it is a head game. No matter what you do, you are fulfilling this "prophecy". No matter how many logical, factual reasons you bring up to show why Jesus cannot be coming back (for example, pointing out the many other false prophecies in the Bible), you are simply fulfilling this "prophecy". If you don't bring up any reasons at all then you are obviously proving, to a Biblical literalist at least, that your silence is agreement. See also False Prophecy #34.

Therefore, here is a prophecy that God just revealed to me. "Thus saith The Lord: The Lord prophesieth that many conservative Christian ministers, seminarians, deacons and elders shalt scoff at what hath been written in 100 False Bible Prophecies. They shalt proclaim that Robert

Collins is wrong. They shalt declare that he taketh verses out of context. They shalt suddenly discover that the translators of the Bible translated it incorrectly and that the Bible does not mean what it clearly says. They shalt contend that Mr Collins is mis-interpreting the Bible, that he is not spiritual enough to understand the Bible, that the devil deceiveth him and the readers, and that thy soul shalt become eternal fondue in the Lake of Fire if thou readest "100 False Bible Prophecies", and believeth what it saith".

The Lord also prophesieth, "The ministers, preachers, pastors and priests who shalt scoff the loudest will be those who are upset because many people who read "100 False Bible Prophecies," will stop donating money to them."

False Prophecy #39

1 John 2:18 says, "Little children, it is the last time: and as ye have heard that antichrist shall come, even now are there many antichrists; whereby we know that it is the last time" (see also 1 John 4:3). According to John, the presence of anti-Christs is supposed to be evidence that "it is the last time". "Antichrist" is defined very broadly only four verses later, in 1 John 2:22, "Who is a liar but he that denieth that Jesus is the Christ? He is antichrist, that denieth the Father and the Son". Everyone who denies that Jesus is the Christ is antichrist, according to the author of 1 John.

The beliefs of every religion are opposed by other religions. Christians are anti-Krishna, anti-Buddha and anti-Tao. Hinduism, Buddhism and Taoism pre-dated Christianity by hundreds of years. These religions, and other first century religions that pre-dated Christianity such as Mithraism, Zoroastrianism, Zeus worship, etc., became anti-Christ as soon as Christianity was created. 1 John 2:18's statement about the "antichrist" is not proof that "this is the last time" or any other "time", because the author knew full well that the vast majority of religions that existed at the time of his writing had existed long before Christianity, and that these religions were by his own definition "antichrist".

The next verse, 1 John 2:19, describes some "anti-Christs": dissenting or apostate Jehovah/Jesus worshippers. "They went out from us, but they were not of us; for if they had been of us, they would no doubt have continued with us: but they went out, that they might be made manifest that they were not all of us."

As with 1 John 2:18, this is nothing new. According to the Bible, people have had theological disagreements since Cain and Abel (Genesis

30

4:2-8). The vast majority of schisms and apostasies in the Bible pre-date the writing of the book of 1 John. A partial list of schisms between God's followers includes Moses, Aaron and Miriam (Numbers 12:1-16), Israel and Judah (1 Kings 11:9-13, 12:16-24), the Corinthian church (1 Corinthians 1:11-17), Judaizing Christians (Acts 15:1-30), and Paul's rebuke of Peter (Galatians 2:11-14). A partial list of apostasies by some of God's followers includes Solomon (1 Kings 11:8), a Corinthian fornicator (1 Corinthians 5:1-5) and disfellowshipped Christians (1 Corinthians 5:11).

1 John 2:18-19 is shrewd psychology, not clairvoyance.

False Prophecy #40

1 John 3:22 predicts, "whatsoever we ask, we receive of him, because we keep his commandments, and do those things that are pleasing in his sight". There are two interpretations of this verse: one is demonstrably untrue and the other is extremely cruel.

The first interpretation is similar to Jesus statement, "And whatsoever ye shall ask in my name, that will I do, that the Father may be glorified in the Son. If ye shall ask any thing in my name, I will do it" (John 14:13-14, see also John 15:7 and 15:16). This belief is contradicted by the multitude of unanswered prayers which are made by sincere Christians who are obedient to God (1 John 3:22), have confessed their sins (1 John 1:9), are asking unselfishly (James 4:3), in Jesus name (John 14:14) and get other Christians to pray with them (Matthew 18:19). For just a few examples, see 1 Chronicles 21:17, 2 Samuel 12:14-18, Luke 8:9-13, John 14:13-14 and Matthew 18:19-20. Even Jesus himself had at least one prayer that was not answered; see John 17:21-23.

The second interpretation is that no human has perfectly kept all of God's commandments, so no human ever gets "whatsoever they ask". Although this has the advantage of being true, it makes 1 John 3:22 a meaningless and cynical "promise". All of your dedication comes to naught because of sins that you committed years ago that you do not even remember, but God holds against you because you did not confess them (1 John1:9). You could get everyone in a dozen megachurches to pray for your critically ill child (2 Samuel 12:15-18), but 1 John 3:22 provides no reason to expect God to answer a single one of those prayers because every one of those thousands of believers disobeyed God at least once in their lives.

It gets worse. If you pray for your child's recovery and he/she dies anyway, it is not God's fault. It is your fault because if you had just confessed more sins, been more dedicated, sincere, generous or whatever, God would have answered your prayers. Imagine how this belief makes parents feel when their child dies! This belief has burdened billions of grieving parents with crushing guilt, and not coincidentally has enriched the church with the tithes and offerings of multitudes of mothers and fathers who were overwhelmed with remorse because they blamed themselves for God not answering their prayers to save their child's life.

When faith ruled, most children, including most Christian children, died before reaching adulthood despite their parents' prayers. Now that humanity has developed scientific medicine, most children of all religions or no religion live many decades into adulthood. Which gives more comfort to the parents of sick children: a minister or priest telling them that it is the will of their best friend (God, John 15:14) for their child to die, or a doctor telling them that if they give medicine to their child that the child will be healed? Penicillin without prayer works better than prayer without penicillin. And penicillin does not cost 10% of your income.

False Prophecy #41

Revelation 21:1-4 says, "I saw a new heaven and a new earth: for the first heaven and the first earth were passed away ... God shall wipe away all tears from their eyes; and there shall be no more death".

But the book of Isaiah says that people will still die after God creates the new heavens and new earth. "For, behold, I create new heavens and a new earth: and the former shall not be remembered, nor come into mind. There shall be no more thence an infant of days, nor an old man that hath not filled his days: for the child shall die an hundred years old" (Isaiah 65:17-20).

False Prophecy #42

Revelation 21:8 predicts, "all liars shall have their part in the lake which burneth with fire and brimstone, which is the second death" (see also Revelation 21:27 and 22:15). This is one of those Bible verses in which "all" definitely does not mean "all".

The Bible's most notable exception to this statement is God himself. 2 Thessalonians 2:11 says, "God shall send them strong delusion, that they should believe a lie". Ezekiel 14:9. "If the prophet be deceived when he hath spoken a thing, I the Lord have deceived that prophet".

In one Bible story, God commanded a spirit to lie. To deceive King Ahab so that he could kill him, "The Lord hath put a lying spirit in the mouth of all these thy prophets" (1 Kings 22:23). The lying spirit was explicitly ordered to lie by God, "go forth, and do so" (1 Kings 22:22, see also1 Kings 22:22-23 and 2 Chronicles 18:21-22). In any court of law, if you command someone to do something wrong, you are as guilty of it as they are.

Bible contains many examples where God rewarded and praised people for lying. Not only did God not object when Hebrew midwives lied to Pharaoh to save the lives of the Hebrew babies, he rewarded them, "Therefore God dealt well with the midwives" (Exodus 1:20).

Rahab lied to keep the men of Jericho from catching Hebrew spies that were hiding in her house. "The king of Jericho sent unto Rahab, saying, Bring forth the men that are come to thee, which are entered into thine house: for they be come to search out all the country. And the woman took the two men, and hid them, and said thus, There came men unto me, but I wist not whence they were" (Joshua 2:3-4). God did not condemn Rahab. God said, "Likewise also was not Rahab the harlot justified by works, when she had received the messengers, and had sent them out another way?" (James 2:25).

Sometimes God punished the wrong people when his followers lied. See Genesis 12:10-20, and 20:1-18.

Jael received God's blessing even though her lie was part of an assassination plot. When Jael invited Sisera to hide in her tent, she said, "turn in to me; fear not" (Judges 4:18). But as soon as Sisera was asleep, Jael took a tent nail and "smote the nail into his temples ... so he died" (Judges 4:21). Not only was Jael not punished, she was given a special blessing in Judges 5:24-27, "Blessed above women shall Jael ... be ... She put her hand to the nail, and her right hand to the workmen's hammer; and with the hammer she smote Sisera".

In 2 Kings 10:18-19, King Jehu actually lied by saying that he would commit idolatry. He did this to lure Baal worshippers so that he could kill them (2 Kings 10:25). Afterwards, "The Lord said unto Jehu, Because thou hast done well in executing that which is right in mine eyes, and hast done unto the house of Ahab according to all that was in mine heart, thy children of the fourth generation shall sit on the throne of Israel" (2 Kings 10:30).

In Exodus 3:18, God commanded Moses to lie by telling Pharaoh that the Israelites only wanted to take a 3-day journey into the wilderness to sacrifice to God. God had already told Moses that he had no intention of letting the Israelites return to Egypt after 3 days. In the verse immediately preceding Exodus 3:18, God said, "I have said, I will bring you up out of the affliction of Egypt unto the land of the Canaanites, and the Hittites, and the Amorites, and the Perizzites, and the Hivites, and the Jebusites" (Exodus 3:17). This command to lie was carried out in Exodus 5:1-3.

False Prophecy #43

In Genesis 4:12 God prophesied to Cain "a fugitive and a vagabond shalt thou be in the earth". The Hebrew word translated "fugitive" in this verse is "nua", which really does mean "fugitive" or "wanderer". It is used in Lamentations 4:14, "They have wandered [nua] as blind men in the streets", and Amos 8:12, "they shall wander [nua] from sea to sea, and from the north even to the east, they shall run to and fro to seek the word of the Lord, and shall not find it". The Hebrew word translated "vagabond" in Genesis 4:12 is "nud". Psalm 11:1 says, "Flee [nud] as a bird to your mountain".

But just 4 verses after Genesis 4:12, the Bible says that Cain did not spend the rest of his life fleeing or wandering, or as a fugitive, vagrant or vagabond. Cain settled down and raised a family. He was even prosperous enough to build a city and name it after his son. "Cain went out from the presence of the Lord, and dwelt in the land of Nod, on the east of Eden. And Cain knew his wife; and she conceived, and bare Enoch: and he builded a city, and called the name of the city, after the name of his son, Enoch" (Genesis 4:16-17).

False Prophecy #44

In Genesis 8:22, God predicted, "While the earth remaineth, seedtime and harvest, and cold and heat, and summer and winter, and day and night shall not cease." But the Bible says that there were famines (i.e., no harvest) in Genesis 41:56 ("the famine was over all the face of the earth"), In Deuteronomy 11:17, God said that if the Israelites were disobedient, "then Jehovah's wrath be kindled against you, and he shut up the heaven, that there be no rain, and that the land yield not her fruit".

False Prophecy #45

Genesis 9:3 says, "Every moving thing that liveth shall be meat for you", but Genesis 7:2-3 says that some animals were "unclean", and other parts of the Bible (Leviticus 11) say that unclean animals must not be eaten. Although Noah preceded the Mosaic Law, he clearly did not precede the concept of "clean" and "unclean" animals, if the Bible is historically accurate.

In addition, there are many "moving things that liveth" that cannot be eaten at all without getting ill and often dying. This includes parasites like tapeworms, schistosomes, liver flukes and dozens if not hundreds of other species of multi-celled parasites, as well as single celled parasites/ pathogens like amoebas and many species of bacteria which move by using flagella. Parasites and pathogens living in the digestive tract kill or sicken millions of people every year.

False Prophecy #46

In Genesis 15:16, God said "But in the fourth generation they [Abraham's descendants] shall come hither again". But Jehovah has already told Abram in Genesis 15:13 that Abram's descendants shall be "in a land that is not theirs" for "four hundred years".

The Hebrew word for "generation" is "dor". A generation is the average time it takes time between the birth of parents and the birth of their offspring, so a generation is at most 33 years. Therefore Genesis 15:13 and Genesis 15:16, only 3 verses apart, disagree with each other by over 250 years.

Psalm 90:10 defines a lifespan as 70-80 years. Some commentators claim that a "generation" [dor] was 100 years, but even today, few people live that long. The Hebrews at that time certainly didn't, because all but two individuals of the generation of adults who left Egypt during the Exodus (Exodus 12) died during their 40 years in the wilderness. (Numbers 32:11-13.)

In addition, the Bible itself reports 6 generations from Abraham to Moses. Abraham fathered Isaac (Genesis 21:1-5), Isaac fathered Jacob/Israel (Genesis 25:19-26), Jacob/Israel fathered Levi (Genesis 35:23), Levi fathered Kohath (Exodus 6:16), Kohath fathered Amram (Exodus 6:18) and Amram fathered Moses (Exodus 6:20).

False Prophecy #47

In Genesis 22:18 and Genesis 26:4, God said to Abraham, "in thy seed shall all the nations of the earth be blessed". But other Bible verses clearly say that there were some nations that definitely were not blessed by Abraham's descendants. They were genocidally exterminated at God's command by Abraham's descendants.

Deuteronomy 20:16-17 says, "But of the cities of these people, which the Lord thy God doth give thee for an inheritance, Thou shalt save alive nothing that breathes. Thou shalt utterly destroy them, namely, the Hittites, and the Amorites, the Canaanites, and the Perizzites, the Hivites and the Jebusites, as Jehovah thy God hath commanded thee" (see also Deuteronomy 7:1-2). This command was ruthlessly carried out in Joshua chapters 10-11.

Deuteronomy 2:30-34 and 3:6 says that the Hebrews "utterly destroyed the men, and the women, and the little ones, of every city, we left none to remain." in Heshbon. Deuteronomy 3:3-6 says that the Hebrews "utterly destroyed them ... utterly destroying the men, women, and children, of every city" in Bashan (see also Numbers 21:33-35). Numbers 21:3 says that the Hebrews "utterly destroyed them and their cities" of the Canaanites at Hormah. 1 Samuel 27:8-11 says, "David smote the land, and left neither man nor woman alive" of the Geshurites, Gezrites, Amalekites.

False Prophecy #48

Genesis 35:10 says, "God said unto him, Thy name is Jacob: thy name shall not be called any more Jacob, but Israel shall be thy name". God violated his own prediction in Genesis 46:2, "God spake unto Israel in the visions of the night, and said, Jacob, Jacob".

False Prophecy #49

Genesis 49:10 says, "The scepter shall not depart from Judah, nor a lawgiver from between his feet, until Shiloh [the Messiah] come". Many commentators regard this as a messianic prophecy (prediction about Christ), and therefore very important. It is also demonstrably untrue.

A "scepter" is a symbol of a sovereign ruler. The Bible says that many Israelite leaders were not descended from Judah.

The Bible says that Moses ruled Israel when they wandered for 40 years, and that he wrote the Old Testament Law contained in the first 5 books of the Old Testament. Moses was descended from Levi (Exodus 4:14).

Joshua took over after Moses. Joshua was descended from Ephraim (Numbers 13:8 & 16), son of Joseph (Genesis 42:51-52).

The second leader of Israel during the time of the Judges was Ehud, descended from Benjamin (Judges 3:15). Gideon, the fifth leader of Israel after Joshua, was descended from Manasseh (Judges 6:15). The sixth leader was Tolah, was descended from Issachar (Judges 10:1). Elon, the twelfth leader, was descended from Zebulon (Judges 12:11). Samson, the thirteenth leader, was descended from Dan (Judges 13:1-25).

The first king of the Israelite nation, selected by God himself (1 Samuel 9:17), was Saul, descended from Benjamin (1 Samuel 9:1-2). Last but not least, the whole nation of Israel was without any king whatsoever, subjugated by foreign rulers, after 586 BCE.

False Prophecy #50

Exodus 12:1-14 describes in detail the ritual of the Passover, and commands God's people "ye shall keep it a feast by an ordinance for ever". God repeated this command in Exodus 12:17 and 12:24.

But most Christians do not celebrate the Passover feast because they do not believe that God wants them to. If "forever" in the Bible is not really forever, it calls into question some of Christians' most cherished beliefs, such as Psalm 9:7, "the Lord shall endure forever", Psalm 37:18, "the Lord knoweth the days of the upright, and their inheritance shall be forever", Psalm 37:28, "the Lord loveth judgment, and forsaketh not his saints, they are preserved forever", Psalm 106:1, "the Lord's mercy endureth forever", and many other passages

False Prophecy #51

In Exodus 15:26, God predicted that if the Israelites obey his laws, "I will put none of these diseases [of the Egyptians] upon thee". This is generally interpreted to mean that if the Hebrews followed Moses' health and dietary stipulations, they would be healthy. But the Bible goes a step further than this; it predicts that they will suffer from none of the diseases that afflicted surrounding nations. There is no evidence that ancient Israelites suffered any less than surrounding nations from malaria, dysentery, smallpox, tuberculosis, polio, epilepsy or many other diseases.

The Mosaic Law requires numerous practices of dubious or even harmful effect, such as avoiding many foods in populations that were often at risk of malnutrition. Yet it says nothing about simple disease preventions like boiling or filtering water before drinking it. It could easily have said, "scratching yourself with cowpox prevents smallpox", "eating fruit prevents scurvy" or "sleeping under a net and staying away from swampy areas reduces the risk of malaria", but it does not.

If keeping the dietary and health provisions of Old Testament Law was so good for you, God would not have told Christians that they no longer had to do it (Acts 10:9-16), unless God wanted Christians to be sicker than Jews.

37

False Prophecy #52

Exodus 20:5 predicts that God will "visit the iniquity of the fathers upon the children unto the third and fourth generation". Exodus 34:7, Numbers 14:18 and Deuteronomy 5:9 say about the same thing. The same Hebrew word for "iniquity" [avon] is used in all of these verses. Jeremiah 32:17-23 is clear that this is not a friendly visit, "Ah Lord God! ... Thou ... recompensest the iniquity [avon] of the fathers into the bosom of their children after them .. therefore thous hast caused all this evil to come upon them".

It is difficult to imagine a statement that is more unjust and even absurd. Many of us cannot even name all of our great-grandparents, but if any of your great-grandparents, grandparents or parents were bad people, God will visit their iniquity on you.

This contradicts Ezekiel 18:20, which says, "The son shall not bear the iniquity [avon] of the father, neither shall the father bear the iniquity [avon] of the son, the righteousness of the righteous shall be upon him, and the wickedness of the wicked shall be upon him".

False Prophecy #53

In Exodus 34:1, God said that he would write the Ten Commandments on the new tablets. "Hew thee two tables of stone like unto the first: and I will write upon these tables the words that were in the first tables, which thou brakest."

But Exodus 34:27-28 says that God told Moses to write the Ten Commandments on the new tablets, "And the Lord said unto Moses, Write thou these words: for after the tenor of these words I have made a covenant with thee and with Israel. And he was there with the Lord forty days and forty nights; he did neither eat bread, nor drink water. And he wrote upon the tables the words of the covenant, the Ten Commandments."

False Prophecy #54

Deuteronomy 15:11 says, "For the poor shall never cease out of the land". But seven verses earlier, Deuteronomy 15:4 says, "Save when there shall be no poor among you; for Jehovah shall greatly bless thee in the land which Jehovah thy God giveth thee for an inheritance to possess it."

False Prophecy #55

Matthew 26:52 says, "Then said Jesus unto him ... all they that take the sword shall perish with the sword". The Bible is very clear that not "all

38

they that take the sword shall perish with the sword".

Moses ordered the massacre of 3,000 Israelites (Exodus 32:27-28), the extermination of tens of thousands of Midianite women and male children (Numbers 31:14-18), commanded the army that "smote ... all his people, until there was none left alive" in 60 cities together with "a great many unwalled towns" in Bashan (Numbers 21:33-35) and "utterly destroyed the men, and the women, and the little ones, of every city, we left none to remain" in Heshbon (Deuteronomy 2:30-34 and 3:6). Yet Moses died peacefully and angels buried him (Deuteronomy 34:1-7, Jude 1:9).

"Joshua had taken Ai, and had utterly destroyed it;" (Joshua 10:1). "Joshua and the children of Israel had made an end of slaying them with a very great slaughter, till they were consumed" (Joshua 10:20). "Joshua smote them, and slew them, and hanged them on five trees" (Joshua 10:26). "Joshua took Makkedah, and smote it with the edge of the sword, and the king thereof he utterly destroyed, them, and all the souls that were therein; he let none remain" (Joshua 10:28). "Joshua smote him and his people, until he had left him none remaining" (Joshua 10:33). "Joshua smote all the country of the hills, and of the south, and of the vale, and of the springs, and all their kings: he left none remaining, but utterly destroyed all that breathed, as the Lord God of Israel commanded. And Joshua smote them from Kadesh-barnea even unto Gaza, and all the country of Goshen, even unto Gibeon. And all these kings and their land did Joshua take at one time" (Joshua 10:40-42). Yet Joshua died peacefully at a ripe old age (Joshua 24:29-30).

David killed 200 Philistines and sexually mutilated their corpses (1 Samuel 18:20-27), committed genocide on the Geshurites, Gezrites, and Amalekites (1 Samuel 27:8-12) and Moabites (2 Samuel 8:2) and ordered the slaughter of people with disabilities (2 Samuel 5:7-10). David murdered Uriah because he had committed adultery with Uriah's wife (2 Samuel 11:1-12:24). Then God said, "Now therefore the sword shall never depart from thine house; because thou hast despised me, and hast taken the wife of Uriah the Hittite to be thy wife." (2 Samuel 12:10); God also killed David's son as punishment (2 Samuel 12:14-18). God would not let David build the temple because, "Thou hast shed blood abundantly, and hast made great wars: thou shalt not build an house unto my name, because thou hast shed much blood upon the earth in my sight" (1 Chronicles 22:8). David lived to be "old and full of days" (1 Chronicles 23:1) and died of natural causes in his own palace where a "fair damsel" had kept him warm (1 Kings 1:1-2:10).

39

History has many other examples of people who did "take the sword" but did not "perish by the sword". These include Stalin, Napoleon, Alexander the Great and many others.

The Greek word translated "all" in Matthew 26:52 is "pas". If "pas" does not really mean "all", it undermines one of Christianity's most important doctrines: the idea that Jesus forgives all of believers' sins. Colossians 2:13 says that Jesus, "having forgiven you all [pas] trespasses". Acts 13:39 says, "by him [Jesus] all [pas] that believe are justified from all [pas] things".

If "all" does not always mean "all" in the Bible, it causes serious problems for people who believe that Jesus died for "all" of the sins that they have committed. Since even a single unforgiven sin can send you to Hell (James 2:10), if you can't be sure that Jesus died for literally "all" of your sins, you can never be sure that you are saved, or even that you can be saved.

False Prophecy #56

Joshua 6:26 says, "Cursed be the man before Jehovah, that riseth up and buildeth this city Jericho: he shall lay the foundation thereof in his firstborn, and in his youngest son shall he set up the gates of it." In other words, Jehovah put a curse on Jericho so that if any man tried to rebuild it, his firstborn son would die while he was laying the foundation, and his youngest son would die while he was building the gates.

This "prophecy" was supposedly "fulfilled" in 1 Kings 16:34, but in doing so, God violated his own law. Deuteronomy 24:16 says, "The fathers shall not be put to death for the children, neither shall the children be put to death for the fathers: every man shall be put to death for his own sin."

False Prophecy #57

Zephaniah 2:9 predicts, "Therefore as I live, saith the Lord of hosts, the God of Israel, Surely Moab shall be as Sodom, and the children of Ammon as Gomorrah, even the breeding of nettles, and saltpits, and a perpetual desolation: the residue of my people shall spoil them, and the remnant of my people shall possess them".

This is a false prophecy. Sodom and Gomorrah are believed to have been next to the Dead Sea, an area which is now uninhabited desert. The territories of Moab and Ammon, however, are in what is now Jordan, a nation with 6 million inhabitants, not a "perpetual desolation". Jordan's capital,

Amman, bears an obvious linguistic connection with the Biblical "Ammon", and is a city of 2 million inhabitants

False Prophecy #58

In Exodus 17:14, God predicted, "I will utterly put out the remembrance of Amalek from under heaven." But Amalek is mentioned over 20 times in the Bible, so we (here on earth, "under heaven") still remember them thousands of years later. The Bible is God's word. Since the Bible says, "the word of our God will stand forever" (Isaiah 40:8), the Amalekites will be remembered forever.

False prophecy #59

In 1 Kings 11:13, God said that he would not take away all of Solomon's kingdom; he "will give <u>one</u> tribe to thy son". In 1 Kings 11:35-36, Jehovah said, "I will take the kingdom out of his [Solomon's] son's hand, and will give it unto thee [Jeroboam, who was not related to Solomon], even ten tribes. And unto his son will I give <u>one</u> tribe, that David my servant may have a light always before me in Jerusalem, the city which I have chosen me to put my name there". 1 Kings 12:20 says, "There was none that followed the house of David, but the tribe of Judah only".

But other passages in the Bible say very clearly that three tribes, Judah, Benjamin and Levi, stayed loyal to the Davidic dynasty. Judah and Benjamin remained under the dominion of Solomon's descendants continually until the deportation to Babylon (1 Kings 12:21, 12:23, 2 Chronicles 11:1, 11:12, 11:23, 14:8, 15:2, 15:8-9, 25:5, 31:1, 34:9, 34:32), and returned to live in Judea and practice Jehovah worship until the end of Old Testament times (Ezra 1:5, 4:1, 10:9, Nehemiah 11:4, 11:31-36). The Benjamites remained in Judea and kept their tribal identity even in New Testament times (Romans 11:1, Philippians 3:5). Some apologists claim that the tribe of Benjamin was so small that it was irrelevant. But 2 Chronicles 14:8 says that in the time of King Asa (Solomon's great-grandson), Judah and Benjamin were about the same size - Judah had 300,000 soldiers and Benjamin had 280,000 soldiers.

2 Chronicles 11:13-14 says that a third tribe, Levi, also remained loyal to the kings descended from David, "The priests and the Levites that were in <u>all</u> Israel resorted to him [Solomon's son Rehoboam] out of <u>all</u> their coasts [Revised Standard Bible "from <u>all</u> places where they lived"]. For the Levites left their suburbs and their possession, and came to Judah and Jerusalem: for Jeroboam and his sons had cast them off from executing the

priest's office unto Jehovah". Levites continued to live in Jerusalem at least until New Testament times (John 1:19).

False Prophecy #60

In 2 Kings 22:20, God promised and predicted, "Behold therefore, I will gather thee [King Josiah] unto thy fathers, and thou shalt be gathered into thy grave in peace." But Josiah's death was anything but peaceful. "Pharaohnechoh king of Egypt went up against the king of Assyria to the river Euphrates: and king Josiah went against him; and he slew him at Megiddo, when he had seen him. And his servants carried him in a chariot dead from Megiddo" (2 Kings 23:29-30, see also 2 Chronicles 35:22-24).

Sometimes, God revoked his promise because of some sin(s) committed by the person to whom the promise was made. (That was what happened to King Zedekiah in Jeremiah 34:4-17.) But 2 Kings 23:1-24 says very clearly that Josiah was faithful to God and describes many reforms that Josiah instituted to bring Judah back into obedience to God. 2 Kings 23:25 says, "Like unto him [Josiah] was there no king before him, that turned to the Lord with all his heart, and with all his soul, and with all his might, according to all the law of Moses; neither after him arose there any like him".

So why did God not fulfill his promise to Josiah? "Notwithstanding the Lord turned not from the fierceness of his great wrath, wherewith his anger was kindled against Judah, because of all the provocations that Manasseh [Josiah's grandfather] had provoked him withal" (2 Kings 23:26).

There are two insurmountable problems with the "explanation" in 2 Kings 23:26. First, Manasseh had repented of his sins (2 Chronicles 33:12-19). The Bible promises that when a person repents, "I [God], even I, am he that blotteth out thy transgressions for mine own sake, and will not remember thy sins" (Isaiah 43:25, see also Jeremiah 31:24). The Bible also promises that God's "anger endureth but a moment" (Psalm 30:5). Although Manasseh had repented and died decades earlier, 2 Chronicles 23:26-30 says that God still remembered Manasseh's sins and was still so angry about them that he broke his promise to his faithful follower Josiah by allowing Josiah to be killed.

Second, the Bible prohibits punishing people for their ancestor's sins. "The fathers shall not be put to death for the children, neither shall the children be put to death for the fathers: every man shall be put to death for his own sin" (Deuteronomy 22:16). Manasseh was Josiah's grandfather

42

(2 Kings 21:18 and 21:25-26), and had been dead for 33 years when Josiah was killed (2 Kings 21:18-19, 22:1).

False Prophecy #61

Jeremiah 36:30 says, "Thus saith Jehovah of Jehoiachim king of Judah; he shall have none to sit upon the throne of David". But 2 Kings 24:6-8 says, "Jehoiachim slept with his fathers; and Jehoiachin his son reigned in his stead ... Jehoiachin was eighteen years old when he began to reign, and he reigned in Jerusalem three months".

False Prophecy #62

In 2 Chronicles 1:12, God told Solomon, "I will give thee riches, and wealth, and honour, such as none of the kings have had that have been before thee, neither shall there any after thee have the like".

There are two problems with this. First, the Bible condemns excessive material wealth. Luke 6:24 says, "woe unto you that are rich! For ye have received your consolation." James 2:5 says, "Hearken, my beloved brethren, Hath not God chosen the poor of this world rich in faith, and heirs of the kingdom which he hath promised to them that love him?"

Second, this verse's claim that Solomon would have "riches, wealth and honor" more than any king after him contradicts the Bible's teaching that Jesus will establish his kingdom on earth. If Jesus comes back and establishes his earthly kingdom, like the book of Revelation says he will, he will certainly be richer than Solomon.

False Prophecy #63

Psalms 1:1-3 predicts, "Blessed is the man that walketh not in the counsel of the ungodly, nor standeth in the way of sinners, nor sitteth in the seat of the scornful. But his delight is in the law of the Lord; and in his law doth he meditate day and night. And he shall be like a tree planted by the rivers of water, that bringeth forth his fruit in his season; his leaf also shall not wither; and whatsoever he doeth shall prosper."

It requires considerable hubris to place these verses immediately after the book of Job, as they are in most Bibles. Job was the most faithful man in the world (Job 1:8, 2:3), but God and Satan destroyed Job's wealth (Job 1:8-17), killed his children (Job 1:18-19, Job 2:3) and struck Job with a horrible disease (Job 2:3-8). To say that Job "delighted" in anything during most of the book of Job is to disbelieve Job's repeated statements of utter misery (Job 3:1-26, 6:1-9, 7:4-21, 9:25-31, 10:1, 10:18-19, 16:1-22, etc.).

For your children to all be killed on the same day is about as opposite as you can get from being "blessed" or "whatsoever he doeth shall prosper".

False Prophecy #64

Psalm 34:20 says, "He keepeth all his bones: not one of them is broken". This is universally regarded as a Messianic prophecy by New Testament believers, because it is referred to in the Gospel of John's record of the crucifixion (John 19:31-36).

The problem is that the verse immediately preceding Psalm 34:20 makes it clear that this passage cannot be talking about the crucifixion of Jesus. "Many are the afflictions of the righteous: but the Lord delivereth him out of them all" (Psalm 34:19). The whole purpose of the crucifixion was that God would not deliver Jesus out of his afflictions on the cross, so that Jesus could be the sacrifice for humanity's sins. Jesus himself is reported to have said, "My God, my God, why hast thou forsaken me?" (Matthew 27:46, Mark 15:34).

False Prophecy #65

Psalm 55:23 predicts, "Bloody and deceitful men shall not live out half their days". But Job 21:7 says, "Wherefore [why] do the wicked live, become old ...?" Ecclesiastes 7:15 says, "there is a just man that perisheth in his righteousness, and there is a wicked man that prolongeth his life in his wickedness".

Psalm 55:23 not only contradicts Job 21:7 and Ecclesiastes 7:15, it is obviously untrue. The average life expectancy today in nations with modern health care is between 70-80 years. If Psalm 55:23 was true, the average life span of "bloody and deceitful" people living in these same nations would be about 35-40 years. Imagine the enormous savings to our prison systems if Psalm 55:23 was true! Instead of spending billions of taxpayer dollars on life sentences for convicted murderers and rapists until they live into their 70's, most of them would die before they reached their mid-40's.

False Prophecy #66

Psalm 62:12 predicts that God, "renderest to every man according to his work". This verse is quoted in Romans 2:6. Also, Colossians 3:25, says "he that doeth wrong shall receive for the wrong which he hath done".

There are several problems with this. First, Ephesians 2:8-9 says, "For by grace are ye saved through faith; and that not of yourselves:

it is the gift of God. Not of works, lest any man should boast". Romans 11:5-6 says, "Even so then at this present time also there is a remnant according to the election of grace. And if by grace, then is it no more of works: otherwise grace is no more grace. But if it be of works, then is it no more grace: otherwise work is no more work". Numerous New Testament verses echo this idea - works cannot save you, you only have to believe. This is called "cheap grace".

Another problem is that the Bible tells many stories of God not punishing the most egregious sins by some of his chosen people. David is the most extreme example (Psalm 3). Solomon is another example (1 Kings 2:13-25). God ignored the mass murder of Israelites by other Israelites (Judges 21:10-12 and Judges chapter 21). Israel's king Ahab committed murder, theft, bearing false witness and idolatry (1 Kings 21:1-26).

In many cases, God not only did not render to someone "according to his work", he punished other people for their sins! David committed adultery with Bathsheba and murdered her husband, but God "punished" David by killing David's son (2 Samuel 12:14-18). David ordered a census, so God killed 70,000 Israelites but did not harm David (see 2 Samuel 24:1-25). Abraham lied to Pharaoh, so God sent great plagues on Egypt (Genesis 12:10-20). Abraham lied to Abimilech, so God made Abimilech's wives infertile (Genesis 20:1-18).

1 Kings 14:13 says that God actually killed a child because "in him there is found some good"!

False Prophecy #67

Psalm 66:18 says, "If I regard iniquity in my heart, the Lord will not hear me". If that is true, then God's definition of "iniquity" excludes committing genocide. The Hebrew word translated "hear" in Psalm 66:18 is "shamea". Numbers 21:3 says, "God hearkened [shamea] to the voice of Israel, and delivered up the Canaanites; and they utterly destroyed them and their cities".

If there is anything more sociopathic than someone who prays and then murders a lot of people, it is someone who thinks that God's answer to their prayer commands them to do so. See Numbers 21:34-35, Numbers 25:3-13, Numbers 31:1-18, Deuteronomy 3:2-6, Joshua 6:1-17, 8:1-26, 10:7-42.

False Prophecy #68

Psalm 69:9 says, "For the zeal of thine house hath eaten me up". The New Testament claims that this is another Messianic Prophecy; it is quoted as one in John 2:17, "His disciples remembered that it was written, The zeal of thine house hath eaten me up". This "prophecy" in Psalm 69 has the advantage of being extremely vague. All it says is that someone is very zealous about God's house. That certainly could be said about many billions of Christians and Jews who have lived during and since Biblical times. Anyone who has ever read the Bible's description of Solomon's temple, or seen a European cathedral or a modern megachurch building, cannot deny that very large numbers of Bible believers are extremely zealous for their houses of worship.

The definitive disproof of this "prophecy" comes from Psalm 69 itself. Even a casual reading of this Psalm proves that this Psalm cannot be talking about Jesus Christ. Psalm 69:5 says, "O God, thou knowest my foolishness; and my sins are not hid from thee". The Bible teaches that Jesus was the exact opposite of foolish or sinful. Psalm 69:13 says, "O God, in the multitude of thy mercy hear me" and Psalm 69:16 says, "Turn unto me according to the multitude of thy tender mercies". If Jesus needed mercy, he could not have paid the price for anyone's sins. Psalm 69:18 says, "Draw nigh unto my soul, and redeem it". If Jesus' soul needed redemption, he could not have redeemed anyone else.

False Prophecy #69

Psalm 69:21 says, "They gave me also gall for my meat; and in my thirst they gave me vinegar to drink". As with Psalm 69:9, this is believed to be a Messianic Prophecy. This "prophecy" was "fulfilled" in Matthew 27:34-48, Mark 15:23-36 and Luke 23:36. It is invalid for the same reasons as Psalm 69:9. (See comments on Psalm 69:9 in False Prophecy #68.) Psalm 69 makes many clear statements which show that it cannot possibly be talking about Christ . Biblical literalists very often accuse anyone who disagrees with them of taking verses "out of context", i.e., claiming that the verse says something that is clearly contradicted by surrounding verses. But Biblical literalists themselves take this verse very badly out of context when they claim that it is referring to Jesus Christ.

This prophecy was supposedly "fulfilled" when Jesus was offered gall and vinegar while he was on the cross paying the price for humanity's sins. The belief that Christ's death on the cross made it possible for God to forgive humans is absolutely central and essential to the beliefs of all

Christians. Also, the Bible makes it clear that when Jesus was on the cross he wanted God to forgive people, "Father, forgive them; for they know not what they do" (Luke 23:34).

But many statements in Psalm 69 show very clearly that the Psalmist wanted the exact opposite of forgiveness towards those who gave him gall and vinegar, beginning in the very next verse after Psalm 69:21 and continuing for several verses afterwards.

- "Let their table become a snare before them: and that which should have been for their welfare, let it become a trap" (69:22)
- "Let their eyes be darkened, that they see not" (Psalm 69:23)
- "Pour out thine indignation upon them" (Psalm 69:24)
- "Let thy wrathful anger take hold of them" (Psalm 69:24)
- "Let their habitation be desolate" (Psalm 69:25)
- "Add iniquity unto their iniquity" (Psalm 69:27)
- "Let them not come into thy righteousness" (Psalm 69:27)
- "Let them be blotted out of the book of the living" (Psalm 69:28)
- "And not be written with the righteous" (Psalm 69:28)

False Prophecy #70

Psalm 103:8-9 predicts that "The Lord ... neither will he keep his anger for ever" (see also Psalm 30:5). The Hebrew word translated "anger" in Psalm 103:8-9 is "aph". The Hebrew word translated "for ever" in Psalm 103:9 is "olam".

Jeremiah 17:4 says, "For ye have kindled a fire [aph] in mine anger, which shall burn for ever"[olam]

False Prophecy #71

Psalm 118:22 says, "The stone which the builders refused is become the head stone of the corner". This is universally regarded as a Messianic Prophecy by all New Testament believers because it is quoted as one in 1 Peter 2:7.

1 Peter 2:7 takes Psalm 118:22 badly out of context because Psalm 118:22 cannot possibly be talking about Jesus Christ. The verse immediately preceding Psalm 118:22 says, "I will praise thee: for thou hast heard me, and art become my salvation" (Psalm 118:21). If Jesus needed salvation, he could not have saved anyone else

False Prophecy #72

Ezekiel 23:25-26 says, "I [God] will set my jealousy against thee, and they shall deal furiously with thee: they shall take away thy nose and thine ears; and thy remnant shall fall by the sword: they shall take thy sons and thy daughters; and thy residue shall be devoured by the fire. They shall also strip thee out of thy clothes".

The belief that God is jealous is repeated many times in the Bible. For example, Exodus 20:5 says "I the Lord thy God am a jealous God". Exodus 34:14 says, "The Lord, whose name is Jealous, is a jealous God". See also Deuteronomy 4:24, 5:9, 6:15, Joshua 24:19, Nahum 1:2, and Exodus 20:5.

But I Corinthians 13:4 says that love is not jealous. If love is not jealous, and God is jealous in his relationship with believers, how can God claim to truly love believers?

False Prophecy #73

Psalm 128:1-2 predicts, "Blessed is every one that feareth the Lord; that walketh in his ways. For thou shalt eat the labour of thine hands: happy shalt thou be, and it shall be well with thee". Throughout history, this has very often not been true. Before the Industrial Revolution, famines were widespread and frequent, and made no distinctions between Protestant, Catholic, Jew, Muslim, Hindu, or anyone of any other religious belief. It was not at all unusual for Christians and Jews to plant their crops then see "the labor of their hands" wither in drought, be consumed by disease or insects, destroyed or stolen by marauding armies or brigands, washed away by abnormally strong rains, or confiscated as "taxes", "tithes" or various frauds by corrupt officials. Then those who labored to grow those crops starved to death in huge numbers.

The Bible says that God knows that his followers do not always "eat the labour of their hands". That is why God said, "Go to now, ye rich men, weep and howl for your miseries that shall come upon you ... Behold, the hire of the labourers who have reaped down your fields, which is of you kept back by fraud, crieth: and the cries of them which have reaped are entered into the ears of the Lord of sabaoth ... Ye have condemned and killed the just; and he doth not resist you (James 5:1, 5:4 and 5:6).

False Prophecy #74

Psalm 145:10 predicts, "All thy works shall praise thee, O Lord". The Hebrew word translated "praise" in Psalm 145:10 is "yadah".

But Isaiah 38:18 says, "The grave cannot praise [yadah] thee". The Bible says that God created everything (John 1:3, Psalm 146:6), but at

48

least one of God's works cannot praise him: the grave.

This is particularly significant because the Hebrew word translated "all" in Psalm 145:10 is "kol", which is the same word used just a few verses later where God promises, "the Lord preserveth all [kol] them that love him: but all [kol] the wicked will he destroy" (Psalm 145:20). In addition, Psalm 103:3 says that God " ... forgiveth all [kol] thine iniquities". If "all" does not always mean "all" in the Bible, then it calls into question whether God is going to forgive "all" of his followers' sins.

False Prophecy #75

Proverbs 4:10-11 says, "Hear, O my son, and receive my sayings; and the years of thy life shall be many. I have taught thee in the way of wisdom" (see also Proverbs 4:20-22, 9:11 and 10:27). One can only wonder just how much Solomon told his children about vaccination, antibiotics, the germ theory of disease, antiseptics, disinfectants, sterilization of medical instruments and bandages, avoiding toxins such as lead in eating utensils, pipes and paint, how to prevent epidemics by control of vermin and proper treatment of sewage, how to prevent water-borne diseases by boiling, prevention of mosquito-borne diseases like Yellow Fever and Malaria, or how to prevent scurvy, rickets and protein deficiencies by knowing how to make meals that are rich in vitamins, minerals and protein. All of that modern knowledge has made dramatic improvements in human health and provided "many" more "years of thy life" for the vast majority of the human race, but not one bit of this knowledge is mentioned in the Bible.

From pre-history through Biblical times and until over 1500 years after the Bible was completely finished, infant and child mortality were so high that most people did not live to adulthood, and an adult was an old man or woman by the time they were 50 years of age, if they did not die before then from diseases that we never even hear about today. It was not until scientifically based health care began to be developed that most people lived past their teens. Now most people live long enough to see their grandchildren.

Although Proverbs 4:10 promises that if we "receive" God's "sayings" then "the years of thy life shall be many", Ecclesiastes 7:15 says, "there is a just man that perisheth in his righteousness, and there is a wicked man that prolongeth his life in his wickedness".

Modern medical wisdom and knowledge have tripled "the years of thy life", i.e., the length of the average human life span. Penicillin without prayer works better than prayer without penicillin. Yet the Bible still claims that its wisdom is better than ours (1 Corinthians 1:19-27, 3:19-20).

False Prophecy #76

Proverbs 17:5 predicts, "He that is glad at calamities shall not be unpunished". The Hebrew word translated "calamity" in this verse is "ed". In Proverbs 1:26, God's Wisdom said, "I also will laugh at your calamity [ed]; I will mock when your fear cometh". See also Psalm 52:5-6.

False Prophecy #77

Isaiah 9:17 says, "Therefore the Lord ... neither shall have mercy on their fatherless and widows: for every one is an hypocrite and an evil-doer, and every mouth speaketh folly" (see also Isaiah 13:16-18). Isaiah 9:17 gives the excuse that these people are hypocrites and evildoers; the same justification that has been used for uncountable atrocities committed by God's followers ever since this verse was written.

Even this poor excuse breaks down, however, when dealing with very young fatherless children. Were the babies and toddlers of dead Jehovah-worshipping fathers less hypocritical and evil than those of dead pagan fathers? The question is ludicrous. Babies and toddlers don't have the mental ability to make those kinds of moral decisions. Yet God said that he would <u>not</u> have mercy on them.

The Hebrew word translated "fatherless" in Isaiah 9:17 is "yathom". Only a few chapters earlier, God commanded us to "relieve the oppressed, judge [New American Standard Bible says "defend"] the fatherless [yathom], plead for the widow" (Isaiah 1:17). Psalm 10:14 says, "thou [God] art the helper of the fatherless". Psalm 68:5 says that God is "A father of the fatherless". Psalm 146:9 says "God ... relieveth the fatherless [yathom]".

Jesus said, "it is not the will of your Father which is in heaven, that one of these little ones should perish" (Matthew 18:14). We are supposed to believe that it is not God's will for a single little child to perish, but God has already told us that he will not show mercy to large numbers of fatherless children.

False Prophecy #78

Isaiah 14:21 says, "Prepare slaughter for his children for the iniquity of their fathers; that they do not rise, nor possess the land, nor fill the face of the world with cities". The Hebrew word translated "fathers" in Isaiah

14:21 is "ab"; the Hebrew word translated "children" in Isaiah 14:21 is "ben". Deuteronomy 24:16 states, "The fathers [ab] shall not be put to death for the children [ben], neither shall the children [ben] be put to death for the fathers [ab]: every man shall be put to death for his own sin."

The Hebrew word translated "iniquity" in Isaiah 14:21 is "avon". Ezekiel 18:20 says, "The son shall not bear the iniquity [avon] of the father [ab], neither shall the father [ab] bear the iniquity of the son" [ben].

FalseProphecy #79

Isaiah 26:3 says, "Thou [God] wilt keep him in perfect peace, whose mind is stayed on thee: because he trusteth in thee". Of course, no human ever has "perfect peace". No human perfectly keeps their mind "stayed" on God. No human perfectly trusts in God. So this verse often leads to a self-perpetuating cycle of guilt among Bible believers. If a believer does not have perfect peace, it means that they do not have perfect trust in God, which is a sin, so they feel really guilty, so they have even less peace, so they feel even more guilty, ad infinitum.

There was one person whom the Bible says perfectly trusted God and kept his mind perfectly "stayed" on God. That person was Jesus. Yet Jesus often did not "keep" "in perfect peace". Jesus wept (John 11:35). Jesus, "being in an agony he prayed more earnestly: and his sweat was as it were great drops of blood falling down to the ground" (Luke 22:44). Jesus said, "My soul is exceeding sorrowful unto death" (Mark 14:34, see also Matthew 26:38).

False Prophecy #80

2 Timothy 3:12 predicts, "all that will live godly in Christ Jesus shall suffer persecution". But Proverbs 16:7 says, "When a man's ways please the Lord, he maketh even his enemies to be at peace with him".

False Prophecy #81

1 Corinthians 3:8 predicts, "every man shall receive his own reward according to his own labour". But the Bible contains many examples of God punishing the wrong people for sins committed by others and not punishing his followers for extremely serious sins.

In 2 Samuel 24:1-25, David sinned, but God sent a plague on Israel that killed 70,000 people in three days and left David unharmed. In the famous case of David and Bathsheba, God punished other people, not David (see 2 Samuel 11:1-12:24). Abram deceived Pharaoh, so God sent a plague on Egypt, not on Abram (Genesis 12:10-20). Abraham and Sarah deceived Abimelech, king of Gerar, and God "fast closed up all of the wombs of the house of Abimelech" (Genesis 20:1-18), but Abraham actually became wealthier. See Acts 5:1-11.

The Bible also provides many examples of God not punishing some of the most egregious sins. God did not punish King David when he sexually mutilated 200 corpses (1 Samuel 18:20-27), committed genocide on the Geshurites, Gezrites, and Amalekites (1 Samuel 27:8-12), Moabites (2 Samuel 8:2) and Edomites (1 Kings 11:15-16) and ordered the slaughter of people with disabilities (2 Samuel 5:7-10). God did not punish Solomon when he ordered his hit man to assassinate a political enemy (1 Kings 2:13-25). Moses' brother Aaron and sister Miriam both spoke against Moses in the same verses for the same reasons, but God struck only Miriam with leprosy (Numbers 12:1-15). The Israelites murdered almost the entire Israelite tribe of Benjamin and God did not punish them at all (Judges Chapter 21). God let Samson get away with murder (see Judges 14:11-20).

Genocide is probably the most extreme sin that any human can commit. But God did not punish the Israelites at all for the genocidal extermination of the people living in Palestine when the Israelites invaded during Moses' and Joshua's lifetimes. God not only did not punish the Israelites for these mass murders, he commanded the Israelites to commit them. It was not a sin to kill all of those women and children, it was a sin not to. (See Deuteronomy 20:16-18).

False Prophecy #82

Micah 5:2 says, "But thou, Bethlehem Ephratah, though thou be little among the thousands of Judah, yet out of thee shall he come forth unto me that is to be ruler in Israel; whose goings forth have been from of old, from everlasting". This is universally regarded by Christians as a messianic prophecy because it is quoted as one in Matthew 2:5-6 and referenced in John 7:42.

Micah 5:2 cannot possibly be referring to Jesus. The verses immediately following this verse describe a military leader living six centuries before Jesus. "This man shall be the peace, when the Assyrian shall come into our land" (Micah 5:5). "They shall waste the land of Assyria with the sword, and the land of Nimrod in the entrances thereof: thus shall he deliver us from the Assyrian" (Micah 5:6). "The remnant of Jacob shall be among

52

the Gentiles in the midst of many people as a lion ... who ... teareth in pieces, and none can deliver" (Micah 5:8). "Thine hand shall be lifted up upon thine adversaries, and all thine enemies shall be cut off" (Micah 5:9). "I will destroy thy chariots, And I will cut off the cities of thy land, and throw down all thy strong holds" (Micah 3:10-11). "So will I destroy thy cities" (Micah 5:14).

The Assyrian empire was destroyed in 614 BCE and never rebuilt. It wasn't the Jews who destroyed it. Assyria was destroyed by the armies of pagans: Medes and Babylonians. Shortly after conquering the Assyrians, these armies conquered the Jews (2 Kings 24:10-14) looted their temple and installed a puppet king (2 Kings 24:17). About 30 years later, the Babylonians destroyed Jerusalem and deported all but the poorest Jews to Babylon (2 Chronicles 36:5-20, 2 Kings 25:1-21).

False Prophecy #83

Isaiah 42:2 prophesies concerning the Messiah, "He shall not cry, nor lift up, nor cause his voice to be heard in the street". This verse is referenced in Matthew 12:19, "He shall not strive, nor cry; neither shall any man hear his voice in the streets". But Jesus did speak in "the streets" and people did hear him.

Jesus and his disciples were walking to a ruler's house when a woman touched him and he spoke to her (Matthew 9:18-22). While walking with two disciples on the road to Emmaus, Jesus "expounded unto them in all the scriptures the things concerning himself" (Luke 24:13-32).

Some English Bible's translate "strive" and "cry" as "shout", "raise his voice", "make loud speeches". But the Bible clearly says that Jesus spoke to large crowds. One of these crowds had 5,000 men (Mark 6:34-44, Luke 9:11-14). Another had 4,000 people (Mark 8:1-9). It would be impossible for crowds of that size to hear Jesus unless he shouted, raised his voice and made a loud speech

False Prophecy #84

Isaiah 44:24-45:1 says, "Thus saith the Lord ... I am the Lord ... That saith of Cyrus, He is my shepherd, and shall perform all my pleasure. Thus saith the Lord to his anointed, to Cyrus, whose right hand I have holden". Cyrus was the pagan king of Persia. Although he instituted a policy of religious tolerance that allowed the Hebrews and many other groups to return to their native lands, Cyrus never stopped being a pagan.

Yet the Bible claims that "Cyrus ... shall perform all my pleasure".

53

Did Cyrus stop offering sacrifices to Persian gods? No. This clearly violated one of the Top Ten Sins, "Thou shalt not make unto thee any graven image, or any likeness of any thing that is in heaven above, or that is in the earth beneath, or that is in the water under the earth: Thou shalt not bow down thyself to them, nor serve them" (Exodus 20:4-5). Idolatry is arguably the worst sin, a sin to which the author(s) of Isaiah devoted a great amount of effort to condemning (see Isaiah 2:8-9, 2:18-20, 10:10-11, 19:1, 31:7, 44:16, 48:5, 57:4-5, 66:3-4).

So Cyrus only did some of what God wanted, not all. He allowed the Hebrews to build a temple for God in Jerusalem (Ezra 1:1-11), but Cyrus did not do all that God wanted because God wants everyone to not worship idols.

The fact that "all" does not really mean "all" causes serious problems for Bible believers who think that God will forgive all of their sins. The Hebrew word translated "all" in Isaiah 44:28 is "kol", the same word used in Psalm 103:3, which says that God " ... forgiveth all [kol] thine iniquities". In Psalm 145:20, God promised, "the Lord preserveth all [kol] them that love him: but all the wicked will he destroy".

False Prophecy #85

John 19:34-37 says, "One of the soldiers with a spear pierced his side, and forthwith came there out blood and water ... For these things were done, that the scripture should be fulfilled ... And again another scripture saith, They shall look on him whom they pierced".

This is supposedly a "fulfillment" of the prophecy made in Zechariah 12:9-10. "And it shall come to pass in that day, that I will seek to destroy all the nations that come against Jerusalem. And I will pour upon the house of David, and upon the inhabitants of Jerusalem, the spirit of grace and of supplications: and they shall look upon me whom they have pierced, and they shall mourn for him, as one mourneth for his only son, and shall be in bitterness for him, as one that is in bitterness for his firstborn".

John clearly takes this phrase from Zechariah badly out of context. In the verse immediately preceding this phrase, God said that he would "seek to destroy all the nations that come against Jerusalem". But during the crucifixion, Jerusalem was part of a subjugated state under the Roman Empire, and the Romans eventually destroyed it in 67 C.E, the exact opposite of what Zechariah prophesied. In addition, the phrases immediately following the phrase quoted by John predict another event that did not happen at the crucifixion - the Roman soldiers that crucified and pierced Jesus did not mourn for him.

False Prophecy #86

In Jeremiah 19:9, God promised, "I will cause them to eat the flesh of their sons and the flesh of their daughters, and they shall eat every one the flesh of his friend" while Jerusalem was under seige by the Babylonians (see also Leviticus 26:29, Deuteronomy 28:53, Isaiah 9:19-20 and Ezekiel 5:10).

Note that God said he, not anyone else, would cause the Israelites to practice cannibalism. The author of Jeremiah clearly admits what many apologists deny: because God sent the Babylonians to conquer the Hebrews, God himself was responsible for all of the bad things that happened to them.

This macabre prophetic threat, if the Bible is historically accurate, was carried out in Lamentations 2:20 and 4:10. If so, God violated his own law. Deuteronomy 24:16 commands, "The fathers shall not be put to death for the children, neither shall the children be put to death for the fathers: every man shall be put to death for his own sin".

How can anyone possibly claim that God is merciful or just when he causes people to eat their own children? No human court of any nation in the world would dare to give out such a punishment, no matter what hienous crimes were committed. Yet Bible believers claim that the Bible-God's justice is better than man's, and the Bible claims hundreds of times that God is merciful.

How can anyone possibly take seriously the New Testament story, "He [Jesus] took a child, and set him in the midst of them: and when he had taken him in his arms, he said unto them, Whosoever shall receive one of such children in my name, receiveth me: and whosoever shall receive me, receiveth not me, but him that sent me" (Mark 9:36-37), when God sometimes makes people eat children instead of "receiving" them!

False Prophecy #87

Jeremiah 25:11-12 says, "These nations shall serve the king of Babylon seventy years. It shall come to pass, when seventy years are accomplished, that I will punish the king of Babylon, and that nation, saith the Lord, for their iniquity, and the land of the Chaldeans, and will make it perpetual desolations" (see also 2 Chronicles 36:21). This short Bible passage contains four false prophecies.

(1) The Babylonians conquered and deported Judah in 586 BCE. The Babylonians were then conquered in 538 BCE which is only 48 years. Apologists have tried many contortions to arrive at 70 years; none of them work. Their vain attempts include:

- Starting at the first Babylonian deportation in 604 BCE, giving only 66 years This also does not work because the people of Judah rebelled and did not "serve the King of Babylon" from 588-587 BCE (2 Kings 24:20-25:1, Jeremiah 52:3-6).

- Using Ussher's date for the return of the Jews to Jerusalem, 536 BCE, giving 50 years

- Completely ignoring these verses' clear statement that it is talking about the destruction of Babylon. Some commentators say that these verses are really referring to the rebuilding of God's temple in Jerusalem, which supposedly occurred in 516 BCE (Ezra 6:15), 22 years after the fall of Babylon. 586-516=70 years, but this "interpretation" is absolutely contrary to the obvious meaning of Jeremiah 25:11-12.

(2) Although the city of Babylon was destroyed in 538 BCE and gradually faded into obscurity, Jeremiah 25:12 prophesied that not only Babylon, but also "the land of the Chaldeans" shall be "perpetual desolations" (see also Jeremiah 50:39, 51:24-26 and 51:42-43). The Bible itself says that just a few decades later "the land of the Chaldeans" was so prosperous that Jews living in former Babylonian areas sent large amounts of gold and silver to Jerusalem to rebuild God's temple (Ezra 2:68-29, Nehemiah 7:70-71). These lavish donations were given in 536 BCE, just two years after God supposedly let the Assyrians punish the Babylonian nation by making it a perpetual desolation (Ezra 1:1-3:1). Most of the land that had been in the Babylonian nation continued to support large populations as well as agriculture, art, literature and education for thousands of years and today is in modern-day Iraq, which is currently inhabited by about 25,000,000 people.

(3) The Babylonians conquered Judah in 604 BCE and again in 586 BCE. The vast majority of these conquerors were long dead by the time the Babylonian empire fell in 538 BCE. God punished millions of Babylonians who were not even born when Judah was conquered.

(4) Perhaps most importantly, king Nebuchadnezzar and the Babylonians were doing God's will by conquering Judah. Just a few verses earlier, God had actually called Nebuchadnezzar "my servant" (Jeremiah 25:9). Shortly after this verse, God said, "Now have I given all these lands into the hand of Nebuchadnezzar the king of Babylon, my servant"(Jeremiah 27:6,

see also Jeremiah 43:10). To fail to conquer Judah would have been to disobey God's will, but successfully conquering Judah incurred God's punishment. The Babylonians were literally "damned if you do and damned if you don't".

False Prophecy #88

Ezekiel 6:10 says, "And they shall know that I am the Lord, and that I have not said in vain that I would do this evil unto them" (see also Jeremiah 42:10 and Jeremiah 44:2). The Hebrew word translated "do" in Ezekiel 6:10 is "asah". The Hebrew word translated "evil" in Ezekiel 6:10 is "ra", which really does mean "evil" (see 1 Samuel 16:14). In fact, "ra" is used in the very next verse, in a context that can only mean real moral and spiritual evil, "Alas for all the evil [ra] abominations of the house of Israel! for they shall fall by the sword, by the famine, and by the pestilence" (Ezekiel 6:11).

But other Bible passages clearly condemn evil doers. Psalms 34:16 says, "The face of the Lord is against them that do [asah] evil [ra], to cut off the remembrance of them from the earth". Psalm 15:1-3 says, "the Lord, who shall abide in thy tabernacle? who shall dwell in thy holy hill? ... He that backbiteth not with his tongue, nor doeth [asah] evil [ra] to his neighbour". Proverbs 2:14 condemns those "Who rejoice to do evil". Deuteronomy 4:25-26 says, "When ... ye shall have remained long in the land ... and shall do [asah] evil [ra] in the sight of the Lord thy God, to provoke him to anger ... ye shall soon utterly perish from off the land". Judges 3:12 says, "And the children of Israel did [asah] evil [ra] again in the sight of the Lord: and strengthened Eglon the king of Moab against Israel, because they had done [asah] evil [na] in the sight of the Lord".

The New Testament also condemns evil doers. "He that doeth evil hath not seen God" (3 John 1:11). "Every one that doeth evil hateth the light [Jesus]" (John 3:20)."The face of the Lord is against them that do evil" (1 Peter 3:12). The Bible emphatically condemns doing evil even if it produces a good result, "And not rather, as we be slanderously reported, and as some affirm that we say, Let us do evil, that good may come? Whose damnation is just" (Romans 3:8).

False Prophecy #89

Ezekiel 18:14-17 lists a number of things, then predicts that if the son of a sinful person does those things and he "hath executed my judgments, hath walked in my statutes; he shall not die for the iniquity of his father, he shall surely live" (see also Ezekiel 18:20). The Bible gives two very clear contradictions to this assertion.

David committed adultery with Bathsheba, then murdered her husband. This is a very clear and premeditated case of adultery and murder, which earned David two death penalties according to God's law (Genesis 9:6, Exodus 21:12, Deuteronomy 22:22). But God did not kill David. God killed David's son. "Because by this deed thou hast given great occasion to the enemies of the Lord to blaspheme, the child also that is born unto thee shall surely die" (2 Samuel 12:14). "And it came to pass on the seventh day, that the child died" (2 Samuel 12:18).

1 Kings 14:1-18 reports the story of the death of Jeroboam's son Abijah. The Lord said that Abijah would die because Jeroboam "hast done evil above all that were before thee: for thou hast gone and made thee other gods" (verse 9). The Bible makes it clear that Abijah was not being killed because of his own sin, "in him [Abijah] there is found some good thing toward the Lord God of Israel in the house of Jeroboam" (verse 13).

False Prophecy #90

Ezekiel 20:35 says, "And I [God] will bring you into the wilderness of the people, and there will I plead with you face to face". The Hebrew word translated "face" twice in this verse is "panim". The Hebrew phrase translated "face to face" in this verse is "panim al-panim". Ezekiel 20:35 contradicts Deuteronomy 34:10, which says, "There arose not a prophet since in Israel like unto Moses, whom the Lord knew face to face" [panim al-panim].

Also, this chapter describes God's reconciliation with the Israelites (see verses 36-38 and 40-43). But if the Bible is true, a face to face "pleading" with God would not be a reconciliation. It would be fatal to the Israelites, because Exodus 33:20 says, "He [God] said, Thou canst not see my face: for there shall no man see me, and live".

False Prophecy #91

Matthew 27:9-10 misquotes an Old Testament prophecy and attributes the quote to the wrong prophet. The author of Matthew says that the quote came from Jeremiah, but really it is found in Zechariah. Differences are italicized.

Matthew 27:9-10 says, "Then was fulfilled that which was spoken by Jeremy the prophet, saying, *And they took the* thirty pieces of silver, *the price of him that was valued, whom they of the children of Israel did* value, And gave them for the potter's field, as the Lord appointed me".

Zechariah 11:12-13 says, "And I said unto them, If ye think good, give me my price; and if not, forbear. *So they weighed for my price* thirty pieces of silver. And the Lord said unto me, *Cast it unto the potter: a goodly price that I was priced at of them. And I* took the thirty pieces of silver, and cast them to the potter *in the house* of the Lord".

Some commentators claim that Matthew is actually quoting Jeremiah 32:8-10. The Jeremiah passage is so different from Matthew 27:9-10 that any comparison is meaningless. "So Hanameel mine uncle's son came to me in the court of the prison according to the word of the Lord, and said unto me, Buy my field, I pray thee, that is in Anathoth, which is in the country of Benjamin: for the right of inheritance is thine, and the redemption is thine; buy it for thyself. Then I knew that this was the word of the Lord. And I bought the field of Hanameel my uncle's son, that was in Anathoth, and weighed him the money, even seventeen shekels of silver. And I subscribed the evidence, and sealed it, and took witnesses, and weighed him the money in the balances".

False Prophecy #92

Ezekiel 29:9-12 predicts, "The land of Egypt shall be desolate and waste; and they shall know that I am the Lord: because he hath said, The river is mine, and I have made it. Behold, therefore I am against thee, and against thy rivers, and I will make the land of Egypt utterly waste and desolate, from the tower of Syene even unto the border of Ethiopia. No foot of man shall pass through it, nor foot of beast shall pass through it, neither shall it be inhabited forty years. And I will make the land of Egypt desolate in the midst of the countries that are desolate, and her cities among the cities that are laid waste shall be desolate forty years: and I will scatter the Egyptians among the nations, and will disperse them through the countries.".

This prediction was made well over 2,000 years ago and it has never happened.

False Prophecy #93

Acts 2:16-21 quotes Joel 2:28-33 as a fulfilled prophecy. "This is that which was spoken by the prophet Joel; And it shall come to pass in the last days, saith God, I will pour out of my Spirit upon all flesh [many modern translations say "all people" or "all mankind"], and your sons and your daughters shall prophesy, and your young men shall see visions, and your old men shall dream dreams, And on my servants and on my handmaidens I will pour out in those days of my Spirit; and they shall prophesy. And I will shew wonders in heaven above, and signs in the earth beneath; blood, and fire, and vapour of smoke. The sun shall be turned into darkness, and the moon into blood, before that great and notable day of the Lord come. And it shall come to pass, that whosoever shall call on the name of the Lord shall be saved.".

Obviously, the sun has not yet turned into darkness, nor has the moon turned to blood, nor have there been "wonders in heaven above". In fact, modern astronomy has provided some of the most convincing proof that parts of the Bible are not true - the first few chapters of Genesis clearly say that the whole universe was created about 6,000 years ago, but modern telescopes can see stars, galaxies, quasars and other astronomical objects that are millions and even billions of light years away.

It is also obvious that God has never poured out his spirit on all people. Never in human history have more than a quarter of the people living on earth been Christians or Jews.

False Prophecy #94

Malachi 3:1-4 says "Behold, I will send my messenger, and he shall prepare the way before me: and the Lord, whom ye seek, shall suddenly come to his temple, even the messenger of the covenant, whom ye delight in: behold, he shall come, saith the Lord of hosts. But who may abide the day of his coming? And who shall stand when he appeareth? For he is like a refiner's fire, and like fullers' soap. And he shall sit as a refiner and purifier of silver: and he shall purify the sons of Levi, and purge them as gold and silver, that they may offer unto the Lord an offering in righteousness. Then shall the offering of Judah and Jerusalem be pleasant unto the Lord, as in the days of old, and as in former years."

New Testament believers regard this passage as a prophecy about Jesus as the Messiah. Matthew 11:10, Mark 1:2 and Luke 7:27 all claim that John the Baptist fulfilled the part about the "messenger", though Malachi is pretty short on details.

The Gospels also contain numerous references to Jesus going to the Temple, though it would not take much clairvoyance to predict that a Jew would visit the Temple. But the rest of this passage clearly has not happened. To any objective reader, this passage describes events that will happen in quick succession; there is certainly no indication that there is a 2,000 year gap between the first sentence and the rest of the passage. A prophet who is wrong 75% of the time is not much of one. He certainly fails the Bible's own requirement for a prophet of God (Deuteronomy 18:21-22).

False Prophecy #95

Malachi 4:5 says, "Behold, I will send you Elijah the prophet before the coming of the great and dreadful day of the Lord". Matthew 11:12-14, 17:10-13, Mark 9:11-13 claim that John the Baptist was Elijah. But John the Baptist stated that he was not Elijah in John 1:21-26.

Just like Malachi 3:1-4 (False Prophecy #94, above), the second part of this prediction has not come true, and this verse gives no indication that there is a 2,000 year (or greater) gap between the first part and the second part. A weatherman who predicts "it's going to rain then it's going to snow" is not doing anyone much good if he does not mention that there is a six month gap between his two predictions

It gets worse. The very next verse, Malachi 4:6, contradicts the clear teaching of Jesus, "And he shall turn the heart of the fathers to the children, and the heart of the children to their fathers, lest I come and smite the earth with a curse". This contradicts Matthew 10:35-36, where Jesus said, "For I am come to set a man at variance against his father, and the daughter against her mother, and the daughter in law against her mother in law, and a man's foes shall be they of his own household". In Luke 14:26, Jesus said, "If any man come to me, and hate not his father, and mother, and wife, and children, and brethren, and sisters, yea, and his own life also, he cannot be my disciple".

False Prophecy #96

Hosea 1:6 says, "God said ... I will no more have mercy upon the house of Israel". Hosea 2:4 says that God said, "I will not have mercy upon her children; for they be the children of whoredoms". The Hebrew word translated "mercy" in these verses is "racham".

But Psalm 145:9 says, "The Lord is good to all, and his tender mercies [racham] are over all his works".

False Prophecy #97

Hosea 13:16 says, "Samaria shall become desolate; for she hath rebelled against her God: they shall fall by the sword: their infants shall be dashed in pieces, and their women with child shall be ripped up". Hosea 9:16 says, "yea, though they bring forth, yet will I slay even the beloved fruit of their womb" (see also Hosea 9:12 and 9:14).

It is difficult to imagine more explicit and clear statements that God will kill Samarian infants because their parents "hath rebelled against" God. Infants are no more capable of committing idolatry than they are capable of reading the Bible, yet "their infants shall be dashed in pieces".

It gets worse. When God fulfilled his prophecy "their women with child shall be ripped up", fetuses and embryos were destroyed. The Bible explicitly says that fetuses and embryos cannot commit idolatry or any other sin, "children being not yet born, neither having done any good or evil" (Romans 9:11).

God often killed children and infants for their parents' sins, even though Old Testament Law clearly prohibited doing so. "The fathers shall not be put to death for the children, neither shall the children be put to death for the fathers: every man shall be put to death for his own sin" (Deuteronomy 24:16). See also Deuteronomy 20:16-17, Deuteronomy 24:16, Joshua chapters 10-11, 2 Samuel 11:1-12:24, Lamentations 2:11-12, and Lamentations 4:10.

False Prophecy #98

Amos 8:9 predicts, "And it shall come to pass in that day, saith the Lord God, that I will cause the sun to go down at noon, and I will darken the earth in the clear day". Many commentators claim that this is a Messianic prophecy and was fulfilled in Matthew 27:45, "from the sixth hour there was darkness over all the land unto the ninth hour" (see also Mark 15:33 and Luke 23:44).

There are many very good reasons why Amos 8:9 cannot be describing events that happened on the day of the crucifixion. We know that the sun did not really "go down at noon" because that would have been such a remarkable event that it would have been recorded by historians, and there is not one mention of it in any of the contemporary historical records of that time, including those of Josephus, who wrote extensively about Jerusalem and Judea in the first century. (There were no solar eclipses viewable from Judea during the 20-40 C.E. time period; an eclipse was actually impossible at this time because Passover was held at the same time as a full moon.) In addition, sundown was the signal of the start of the Sabbath. The Bible clearly says that the darkness started at the 6th hour, that Jesus died at the ninth hour (Matthew 27:46-50), and that Jesus was buried before the start of the Sabbath (Luke 23:50-56).

The verses surrounding Amos 8:9 predict events that did not happen when Jesus was crucified. Amos 8:3 says, "the songs of the temple shall be howlings in that day, saith the Lord God, there shall be many dead bodies in every place; they shall cast them forth with silence". There were not "many dead bodies in every place"; Matthew 27:52-53 says that the exact opposite happened - dead people rose from their graves. Amos 8:12 says, "they shall wander from sea to sea, and from the north even to the east, they shall run to and fro to seek the word of the Lord, and shall not find it". But the book of Acts reports that the apostles proclaimed the word of God many times in Jerusalem and Judea for many decades after the crucifixion.

The verse which immediately follows Amos 8:9 describes events of which there is no record in the New Testament. "And I will turn your feasts into mourning, and all your songs into lamentation; and I will bring up sackcloth upon all loins, and baldness upon every head; and I will make it as the mourning of an only son, and the end thereof as a bitter day" (Amos 8:10). There is no report that even one of Jesus' followers wore sackcloth or became bald around the time that Jesus was crucified, but Amos predicted "all" would wear sackcloth and "every" head would become bald.

Amos chapter 8 clearly describes mass carnage and permanent desolation. Amos 8:12 says, "they shall fall, and never rise up again". But a mere 40 hours after the crucifixion, on Sunday morning, there was "great joy" (Matthew 28:8) and just a few hours after that, Jesus' disciples were "glad" (John 20:20), because of the resurrection.

False Prophecy #99

Micah 3:11-12 says, "the priests thereof teach for hire, and the prophets thereof divine for money ... Therefore shall Zion for your sake be plowed as a field, and Jerusalem shall become heaps". These verses are taken literally by some smaller religious groups who prohibit paid clergy, a belief which is profoundly unpopular in large and prosperous Bible believing churches, denominations, para-church groups and other "ministries". I can't imagine why.

Micah 3:11-12 notwithstanding, other Bible passages actually require that ministers and religious teachers be well paid. 1 Timothy 5:17-18 says, "Let the elders that rule well be counted worthy of double honour, especially they who labour in the word and doctrine. For the scripture saith, Thou shalt not muzzle the ox that treadeth out the corn. And, The labourer is worthy of his reward" (see also Matthew 10:10, Luke 10:7). 1 Corinthians 9:13-14 says, "Do ye not know that they which minister about holy things live of the things of the temple? And they which wait at the alter are partakers with the alter? Even so hath the Lord ordained that they which preach the gospel should live of the gospel." In the Old Testament, the tithes (10% of the Hebrews income) became the property of the priests.

False Prophecy #100

1 Peter 4:7 says, "The end of all things is at hand". The idea that Jesus' return is imminent is stated in many Bible passages. James 5:8 says, "the coming of the Lord draweth nigh". Hebrews 10:37 says, "yet a little while, and he that shall come will come, and will not tarry". 1 John 2:18 says, "Little children, it is the last time: and as ye have heard that antichrist shall come, even now are there many antichrists; whereby we know that it is the last time". Luke 9:27 says, "I tell you of a truth, there be some standing here, which shall not taste of death, till they see the kingdom of God". Matthew 16:28 says, "Verily I say unto you, There be some standing here, which shall not taste of death, till they see the Son of man coming in his kingdom."

Revelation 1:1 says, "The Revelation of Jesus Christ, which God gave unto him, to shew unto his servants things which must shortly come to pass". Revelation 22:20 says, "He which testifieth these things saith, Surely I come quickly. Amen. Even so, come, Lord Jesus". See also False Prophecy #34.

There can be no doubt that the early church believed that Jesus would return in the very near future. Acts 5:34-35 says, "for as many as were possessors of lands or houses sold them, and brought the prices of the things that were sold, And laid them down at the apostles' feet". A similar idea is stated in 1 Corinthians 7:29-30, which says, "the time is short: it remaineth, that both they that have wives be as though they had none ... and they that buy, as though they possessed not". Few believers will give away all of their possessions if they believe that they or their families are going to be around for decades. Even fewer are going to give up their wives.

In his commentary on 1 Peter 4:7, written around 1706, Matthew Henry said, "The miserable destruction of the Jewish church and nation foretold by our Savior is very near ... Nay, the world itself will not continue very long. The conflagration will put and end to it".

For almost 2,000 years, the New Testament has said that the end of the world was in the very near future. Conservative Bible theologians have kept believers in constant expectation that the end of the universe would happen in their lifetime. Contemporary pulpits echo this mantra. Today, they're still writing books and even making movies about it. We're still waiting.

Index of Bible References

Verse/Passage	False Prophecy #	Page Number
Exodus 12:1-14	50	37
Exodus 12:17	50	37
Exodus 12:24	50	37
Exodus 15:26	51	37
Exodus 17:14	58	41
Exodus 20:5	52	38
Exodus 20:5	72	47
Exodus 20:5	72	47
Exodus 34:1	53	38
Exodus 34:14	72	47
Exodus 34:7	52	38
Ezekiel 5:10	86	55
Ezekiel 6:10	88	57
Ezekiel 18:14-17	9	57
Ezekiel 18:20	89	57
Ezekiel 20:35	90	58
Ezekiel 23:25-26	72	47
Ezekiel 26:7-12	24	18
Ezekiel 29:9-12	92	59
Genesis 4:12	43	34
Genesis 8:22	44	34
Genesis 9:3	45	34
Genesis 13:15	37	28
Genesis 13:17	37	28
Genesis 15:16	46	35
Genesis 17:8	37	28
Genesis 22:18	47	35
Genesis 26:4	47	35
Genesis 28:13	37	28
Genesis 35:10	48	36
Genesis 49:10	49	36
Hebrews 1:5	35	27
Hebrews 10:37	100	64
Hebrews 10:7	36	28
Hosea 1:6	96	61
Hosea 2:4	96	61
Hosea 9:12-16	97	61

Verse/Passage	False Prophecy #	Page Number
Hosea 11:1-2	8	9
Hosea 13:16	97	61
Isaiah 6:9-10	21	16
Isaiah 7:14	7	7
Isaiah 9:17	77	50
Isaiah 9:19-20	86	55
Isaiah 13:16-18	77	50
Isaiah 14:21	78	50
Isaiah 26:3	79	51
Isaiah 42:2	83	53
Isaiah 44:24-25	84	53
Isaiah 53:7	32	24
Isaiah 53:9	19	15
James 5:8	100	64
Jeremiah 17:4	15	13
Jeremiah 19:9	86	55
Jeremiah 22:23	6	6
Jeremiah 25:11-12	87	55
Jeremiah 31:15	5	3
Jeremiah 32:8-10	91	58
Jeremiah 36:30	61	43
Jeremiah 42:10	88	57
Jeremiah 44:2	88	57
Joel 2:28-22	93	59
John 1:21-26	95	61
John 2:17	68	46
John 7:38	23	17
John 7:42	82	52
John 13:18	4	3
John 14:12	25	19
John 14:13-14	26	19
John 14:26	28	21
John 15:25	27	21
John 15:26	28	21
John 16:13-15	28	21
John 19:31-36	64	44
John 19:34-37	85	54

Verse/Passage	False Prophecy #	Page Number
Joshua 6:26	56	40
Joshua 24:19	72	47
Lamentations 2:20	86	55
Lamentations 4:10	86	55
Leviticus 26:29	86	55
Luke 1:32	20	16
Luke 7:27	94	60
Luke 8:10	21	16
Luke 9:27	100	64
Luke 11:29	2	1
Luke 11:29-30	1	1
Luke 23:36	69	46
Luke 23:43	22	17
Luke 23:44	98	62
Malachi 1:4	15	13
Malachi 3:1-4	94	60
Malachi 4:5	95	61
Mark 1:2	94	60
Mark 8:11-12	2	1
Mark 8:31	14	13
Mark 9:11-13	95	61
Mark 14:25	16	14
Mark 15:23-26	69	46
Mark 15:33	98	62
Mark 16:17-18	18	14
Matthew 1:11-12	6	6
Matthew 1:23	7	7
Matthew 2:12-18	5	3
Matthew 2:14-15	8	9
Matthew 2:23	3	3
Matthew 2:5-6	82	52
Matthew 5:18	9	9
Matthew 5:22	10	10
Matthew 11:10	94	60
Matthew 11:12-14	95	61
Matthew 12:19	83	53
Matthew 16:28	100	64

Verse/Passage	False Prophecy #	Page Number
Psalm 69:4	27	21
Psalm 69:9	68	46
Psalm 103:8-9	70	47
Psalm 118:22	71	47
Psalm 128:1-2	73	48
Psalm 145:10	74	48
Revelation 1:1	100	64
Revelation 20:1-15	15	13
Revelation 21:1-4	41	32
Revelation 21:27	42	32
Revelation 21:8	42	32
Revelation 22:15	42	32
Romans 1:3	31	24
Romans 2:5-6	33	25
Romans 2:6	66	44
Romans 9:11	97	61
Zechariah 11:12-13	91	58
Zechariah 12:9-10	85	54
Zephaniah 2:9	57	40

Appendix 1

False Messianic Prophecies Listed in 100 False Bible Prophecies

A "Messianic Prophecy" is an Old Testament prophecy that was supposedly fulfilled by Jesus Christ.

Verse	False Prophecy #	Page Number
1 Chronicles 17:12-13	35	23
1 Peter 2:7	71	47
2 Samuel 7:13-15	35	27
Acts 1:16-20	29	22
Acts 2:25-27	30	23
Acts 2:30	31	24
Acts 8:32	32	24
Amos 8:9	98	62
Genesis 22:18	47	35
Genesis 26:4	47	35
Genesis 49:10	49	36
Hebrews 1:5	35	7
Hebrews 10:7	36	28
Isaiah 6:9-10	21	2
Isaiah 7:14	7	7
Isaiah 42:2	83	53
Isaiah 53:7	32	24
Isaiah 53:9	19	15
Jeremiah 22:30	6, 20	6,16
Jeremiah 31:15	5	3
Jeremiah 32:8-10	91	5,8
John 7:38	23	17
John 7:42	82	52
John 13:18	4	3
John 15:25	27	21
John 19:31-36	64	44
John 19:34-37	85	54
Luke 7:27	94	60
Luke 8:10	21	16
Luke 23:36	69	46
Luke 23:44	98	62

Verse/Passage	False Prophecy #	Page Number
Malachi 3:1-4	94	60
Malachi 4:5	95	61
Mark 1:2	94	60
Mark 9:11-13	95	61
Mark 15:23-36	69	46
Mark 15:33	98	62
Matthew 1:11-12	6	6
Matthew 1:23	7	7
Matthew 2:12-18	5	3
Matthew 2:14-15	8	9
Matthew 2:23	3	3
Matthew 2:5-6	82	52
Matthew 11:10	94	60
Matthew 11:12-14	95	61
Matthew 12:19	83	53
Matthew 17:10-13	95	61
Matthew 27:34-48	69	46
Matthew 27:45	98	62
Matthew 27:57-60	19	15
Matthew 27:9-10	91	60
Micah 5:2	82	52
Psalm 16:10	30	23
Psalm 34:20	64	44
Psalm 35:19	27	21
Psalm 40:7	36	28
Psalm 41:9	4	3
Psalm 69:21	69	46
Psalm 69:25	29	22
Psalm 69:4	27	21
Psalm 69:9	68	46
Psalm 109:8	29	22
Psalm 118:22	71	47
Zechariah 11:12-13	91	60
Zechariah 12:9-10	85	54

Appendix 2

False Prophecies Spoken By Jesus Himself

Verse	False Prophecy #	Page Number
John 7:38	23	17
John 13:18	4	3
John 14:12	25	19
John 14:13-14	26	19
John 15:25	27	21
John 16:13-15	28	21
Luke 11:29-30	1, 2	1
Luke 23:43	22	17
Luke 8:10	21	16
Mark 8:11-12	2	1
Mark 8:31	14	13
Matthew 5:18	9	9
Matthew 5:22	10	10
Matthew 12:38-40	2	1
Matthew 12:40	1	1
Matthew 16:4	1, 2	1
Matthew 18:19-20	12	12
Matthew 19:28	13	13
Matthew 25:41	15	13
Matthew 26:29	16	14
Matthew 26:34	17	14
Matthew 26:52	55	38
Revelation 22:20	100	64

Appendix 3

Sources

All Bible quotes are from the King James Bible unless otherwise noted. Text in brackets [ ] was added by the author when a brief amplification or clarification was needed. Some portions have been italicized or underlined by the author for emphasis.

Greek and Hebrew translations and transliterations are from Young's Analytical Concordance to the Bible. This concordance was compiled by Robert Young and first printed in 1884. It is one of the most complete, best known and most widely used concordances. Many reproductions of this concordance are still in print.

Abbreviations Used In This Book

BCE - Before the Common Era. This is more accurate than "BC" ("Before Christ") because even most conservative Bible scholars now acknowledge that King Herod died in 4 BC, leading to the theologically disturbing conclusion that Jesus would have been born at least 4 years "Before Christ" (Matthew 2:1-19).

CE – In the Common Era. The method of counting years that is currently used in the industrialized world. This is more accurate than "AD" ("Anno Domini", i.e., "The Year of the Lord") for reasons explained in BCE, above.

JB - Jerusalem Bible

KJB – King James Bible

NASB – New American Standard Bible, copyright 1960-1971 by the Lockman Foundation.

NIB - New International Bible

RSB – Revised Standard Bible

OT - Old Testament

SEP - Septuagint (ancient Greek translation of the OT)

TAN - Tanakh (Hebrew - English parallel Old Testament)

TEB - Today's English Bible, also called Good News For Modern Man or The Good News Bible

Ten Questions to Ask Your Minister, Pastor or Priest

1. It is wrong to kill anyone because of their religion. It is also wrong to kill children because of anything their parents did (Deuteronomy 24:16). So why did God order the murders of large numbers of children and even babies because of their parents' religions (Deuteronomy 20:16-17, Joshua chapters 10-11, 1 Samuel 15:2-3, Numbers chapter 31)?

2. Jesus promised, "I say unto you, if two of you shall agree on earth as touching any thing that they shall ask, it shall be done for them of my Father which is in heaven. For where two or three are gathered in my name, there I am in the midst of them" (Matthew 18:19-20, see also John 14:13-14). The Bible also promises that God "healeth all thy diseases" (Psalm 103:2-3). So why does penicillin without prayer work better than prayer without penicillin?

3. Jesus' version of the Golden Rule commands us, "All things whatsoever ye would that men should do to you, do ye even so to them" (Matthew 7:12). So, imagine you were Jesus and Jesus was you. Would Jesus want you to send him to burn forever in Hell just because he did not believe in you? Would Jesus want you to send hurricanes, tornadoes, earthquakes and tsunamis that kill people?

4. If God sends the Holy Spirit to teach believers what the Bible means (John 16:13-15), why do sincere Bible believers disagree about major doctrines so strongly that they have formed separate denominations such as Baptist, Catholic, Methodist, Presbyterian, Pentecostal, Lutheran, Seventh Day Adventist, etc, in violation of God's command (1 Corinthians 1:10-17, 3:3-7, 11:18-19, Ephesians 4:3-6)?

5. The Bible commands us humans to forgive anyone who sins against us (Matthew 18:21-22). So if someone does not believe what we say, we are commanded to forgive them. But if someone does not believe what God says, they will burn forever in Hell (John 3:18). If someone speaks against us, we are commanded to forgive them (Matthew 5:44), but if someone speaks against the Holy Spirit, God will not forgive them (Matthew 12:32). Isn't God asking us to be more forgiving than he is?

6. If God inspired the writers of the original manuscripts of the Bible to write perfect originals, then why did God allow those manuscripts to be lost and why did God not also inspire the copyists of ancient Bible manuscripts to make perfect copies?

7. God said he loves us (John 3:16). God also said that love is not jealous (1 Corinthians 13:4). So why did God also say "The Lord, whose name is Jealous, is a jealous God" (Exodus 34:14, see also Exodus 20:5 and Ezekiel 23:25)? God sometimes gets so jealous that he cuts off people's noses and ears (Ezekiel 23:25-26), makes them eat their own children (Jeremiah 19:9, Ezekiel 5:9-10), and threatens to do many other horrible things to his followers if they do not do what he says (Deuteronomy 28:15-68). Isn't that a really sick form of "love"?

8. Why does God make billions of people suffer just because thousands of years ago one ancestor ate something he wasn't supposed to (Genesis 3:1-24, Romans 5:12).

9. If people who have never heard about Jesus are not condemned (Romans 2:14-15), then why tell them?

10. Why does the Bible promise a blessing to someone who smashes little babies' heads against rocks (Psalm 137:9)?